WINNING
THE GAME
OF LIFE

WINNING THE GAME OF LIFE

THE SEVEN LESSONS YOU NEVER LEARN IN SCHOOL

BARRY GARAPEDIAN

Cover Design by Nathaniel Roy
Interior Layout and Design by Alice Briggs

ISBNs:
979-8-89165-191-3 *Ebook*
979-8-89165-192-0 *Paperback*
979-8-89165-193-7 *Hardcover*

Published by:
Streamline Books
Kansas City, MO
www.streamlinebookspublishing.com

DEDICATION

This book is dedicated to my incredibly supportive wife and partner in life, Shay-Shay, and my two strong and bold kids, Missy Lou (my daughter), and Scotty (my son), who all keep me honest, grounded, and inspired.

CONTENTS

PREFACE

MY FATHER WAS a journalism professor who believed each of his students had a unique gift. If he could help them hone their skills and enhance their confidence, then each would have the ability to go out into the world and make a real difference.

So many of them did. Many became photojournalists for mainstream newspapers, managing editors for national news magazines, writers for television news networks, and publicists and assistants to politicians holding major offices. Many of these students would come back years later to say to my father, thank you. Thank you for believing in me.

The secret of my dad's success—as a teacher and as a father—was to listen. But more than listen, he tried to *see* them in a much wider context. To him, they were not just students—they were people in their family, citizens in their community and world. He wanted to know their personal journey: what had led them to his classroom. He taught at a community college, so many of his students had day jobs and had to take time off to attend college. He witnessed a lot of personal sacrifice and financial struggle. For many of these students, getting a degree wasn't easy.

My father didn't want any of them to give up, however difficult their journey was. So he encouraged them, listened, and tried to really *see* them—for the whole individuals they truly were.

I believe that is the core of my work. To help people manage their finances, their investments, and their retirement, I have, in my thirty-nine-year career, applied my unique skills to help people.

It's always been about more than growing their money. Like my father, I have seen my clients in a wider context—as parents, siblings, sons, and daughters. As members of their community and their religious institutions. As people wanting to be healthy and fit. I have helped them manage their money by seeing the *whole* of them—their family dynamics, ethical values, and physical and mental well-being.

Like my father, I try to see the whole person and connect with my client in a personally professional way. I know that each of my clients has a unique journey—and it is up to me, their adviser, to help them along their way. Sounds easy, right?

How do you do that?

That's what this book is all about.

PART 1

WHY CREATE VALUE?

DON'T FOLLOW THE PACK: FIND OUT WHAT THE 1% HIGH PERFORMERS ARE DOING

Literally within the first month of my career on Wall Street, I made a list of the top ten producers around the country. I called them up to ask if I could come out and visit them, spend an hour or two in their office. "Could I shadow you?" I asked each one. "You would not have to talk to me—not a single word."

All ten agreed.

I knew there was no way I could replicate what any of them were doing, of course, but I also knew I could learn. I could watch how they spoke to their clients, how they motivated their team, how they spent their time, how they dressed, and even how they arranged the furniture in their office. I could take away ideas to create my own culture. And I could use all that to springboard myself into a great career.

So, on my own dime, I flew out to Chicago. I flew out to St. Louis. I flew out all over the country and met with the literal top producers in the US.

It was extremely motivating.

I'll give you an example. This was 1980s New York, and everyone had huge Bunker computers on their desks. Compared with today's slick, relatively unobtrusive tech, these things were like desktop skyscrapers that everyone always had sitting squarely in front of their face. Imagine trying to connect—or just trying to make eye contact—around a two-foot-tall, almond-colored high-rise of a computer.

Then during one of my shadowing sessions, I met a gentleman who had his computer placed *behind* him, so he wasn't distracted from conversations with his clients by watching second-to-second market fluctuations. I was instantly intrigued. This gentleman focused on making phone calls and connecting with people. His day wasn't about his computer—it was about his clients.

From that day on, my own computer was always behind me.

A BEGINNER'S GUIDE TO POSITIVE DISRUPTION

After that initial battery of transcontinental shadow sessions, I began thinking a lot about all the different ways I could apply my self-aggregated C-suite education to build something of significance—something that would not only give me the life I wanted, but that would also positively impact the lives of others. There are givers and takers in this world, and I had decided early on that my identity was *giver*. I wanted success and growth for everyone in my orbit.

I would need to differentiate myself, and that required plans, strategies, and goals.

Right out of the gate, I focused on utilizing my time as effectively as possible. A lifetime of sports, music, and magic lessons had given me a true fondness for time management; in fact, following a schedule has always been something I enjoy. I relished the chance to implement that love in my career and to find creative ways to maximize the impact of every second of my day.

Between 1997 to 2001, I never drove a car. I'd been spending an hour to two hours a day driving in and out of the city. I wondered if there was more I could do with that block of time. I concluded it could be better spent if I wasn't the one behind the wheel, so I bought a Lincoln town car—a limo—and hired a personal driver to pick me up at my home and drive me into the city. At the time, no one I knew was utilizing their drive in that way or maximizing efficiency to that degree.

My focus on utilizing time efficiently also led me to hire callers to dial and connect my calls. That's right—I never punched a button or dialed a phone. It wasn't that I was "above" that work or any such nonsense. It was that I knew my time had more value being spent *on* a call than attempting to keep someone from hanging up before I had the chance to speak.

Before I hired my team of callers, I read up on studies coming out at the time. These studies suggested that caller's voices with specific characteristics created a higher probability that a cold call recipient would stay on the line. Suffice it to say, I leaned into the research, which identified female voices with British or South African accents as those most likely to retain a call.

Yes—I hired individuals with those characteristics.

"Hold for Mr. Garapedian, please," they would say when the call recipient answered, and then they would transfer the call to me. I was always ready to give my pitch, knowing I had prepared for a number of objections a person might have. The hard part—getting them on the phone in the first place—was behind me, thanks to my connectors, and I made sure I was well-versed in the twelve most common objections to my pitch. I rehearsed what I planned to say, so the conversations played out organically.

Making initial connections to build my client base took a lot of creativity. Three of my hired cold callers even made calls for me in the evening. At the same time, I sent out around two thousand pieces of mass mail a week describing new ideas related to my business. I also tasked my wife with running a computer that made around seven hundred robocalls a day. (Remember, this was the eighties and nineties, before these types of calls were outlawed, and when tactics like robocalls and mass mailers were novel enough that they actually worked.)

Besides tactics for making calls, there were other things I did differently early in my career. I created a digital dashboard of practices I needed to do that were activity driven rather than results driven. What that meant for me was that I was historically the first person to come into the office in the morning. I always arrived at 5:00 a.m.—and out on the Pacific coast, *no one* was working that early. "First to the office and last to leave" might be a common adage in business these days, but what made me different was that I didn't do it to gain a specific result. The activity, the *practice* of coming in early day in and day out, was the point.

That doesn't mean I wasn't paying attention to the numbers. On that same dashboard, I also had around eight to ten different metrics I was measuring at any given time. These included things like how often I arrived early to the office, the number of phone calls I was making, how many handwritten notes I was sending out, the amount of money I found in potential clients' assets, how much I was asking for an order...the list went on.

By the middle of my career, I had become even more creative in my methods for establishing myself as a stand-out individual in my field. I created value by sending elaborate handwritten notes (a tactic that I'll detail for you in chapter 5). I perfected my technique in the eighties and nineties, before cell phones and video texts ruled interpersonal communications but after personalized, handwritten notes were becoming increasingly rare. I went the extra mile to send value in a handwritten birthday card, sometimes including an invitation to the very exclusive nightclub in Hollywood known as the Magic Castle. No one I knew was doing that, that's for sure.

I also prioritized *fun*. I conceptualized incredibly engaging, sophisticated dinner parties, which I called Dash Dinners. I would invite fifteen to eighteen influential individuals, people I knew I could connect. We never talked about business; we just had an absolute blast. I'll describe these dinners in more detail in chapter 3 as one of my eighteen tactics. For now, it's enough to point out that the crux of these events was their emphasis on having fun and making genuine connections.

You could say they were my way of moving the Bunker off my desk and putting it behind me.

THE VALUE IN HAVING A PLAN

As my career progressed, I soon learned the two biggest stressors of Wall Street clients: confusion and fear. Thus I made my narrative such that I could dispel and mitigate the two by providing my clients clarity and transparency in the form of a plan.

I began by taking the time to explain to them that creating a customized, workable plan for each client was part of our protocol—the heart of working with us. It sounds simple, but offering a clear path forward was invaluable. With their goals and benchmarks laid out for them in black and white, clients found it easier to relax and become confident. It gave them the kind of hope that allowed them to move forward into the future they dreamed of but feared they would never be able to attain.

Hope is a powerful motivator. Consider a client who wants to buy a house but feels like it's outside of their reach or resources to do so. I could come in with a particular strategy that would allow them to reach that goal and show it to them on paper.

I often used what Dan Sullivan, founder and president of the Strategic Coach, called a "strategy circle." First, I divided a circle into four quadrants. On the top left, I articulated the client's goal: in this example, to buy a house. On the top right, I listed their time horizon—the date we wanted to accomplish the goal. On the bottom left, we listed concerns and obstacles. Finally, on the bottom right, we offset each obstacle with its solution. An obstacle could be, "Where will we buy a house?" and its solution might be, "Enlist a real estate broker."

A common obstacle I saw was, "We don't have enough money for a down payment." But when I came in with a plan for saving a certain percentage of my client's income each month and showed them exactly how many months it would take to save their down payment, they suddenly had hope that they could buy. I used the same strategy to help clients save for college, graduate school—you name it. And it really helped my clients see and understand that these big financial investments were accessible to them.

By creating a plan, I was able to create a kind of value my clients simply weren't getting anywhere else.

DREAMING BIG

Dreaming big is all about self-belief and confidence. I have always been big on the power of being positive, maintaining a can-do attitude, and creating a vision of where my clients want to be in the future.

To do all that, I use four questions: Where were you? Where are you now? Where do you want to be? How are we going to get there? Taking my clients through this process of discovery ultimately made it possible for me to give them the tools they needed to secure the future they'd always dreamed of having. For instance, I was able to use someone's yearly salary of $200,000 and give them a strategy for savings, a high single-digit return that factored in their risk tolerance to distribute their money in equities and, say, fixed-income bonds, and even differentiated equities for the returns that would get them where they wanted to be.

For me, dreaming big always involves visualization. When I think of dreaming, I think about how much I always loved asking my finance clients what their dreams were because so many of them didn't yet have a vision. I was there to help them create one.

A person needs to see their dream laid out in a physical medium for it to seem like a real possibility. Imagery is powerful—what we see becomes what we prioritize becomes what our goals are becomes what our reality looks like. The process, I think, is subliminal. Seeing an image of the thing I want reminds me that if I'm not working hard, or doing X, Y, Z parts of the plan, I'm never going to get it. *How am I going to get this home if I am sitting here waiting for something to happen?* I'll wonder. A picture helps remind me to get off my rear and make things happen. It is a natural source of inspiration for me.

I encouraged my clients to take pictures and tape them to their computers. "Is there a car you want to buy or a certain style of house you want to own? Find a picture of that white picket fence and put it somewhere you'll see it," I'd say. Sometimes those pictures did go on their computers. Other times they went in a "goals book" or, eventually, on a vision board. Wherever the pictures landed, dreaming through imagery helped my clients home in on their goals.

THE VALUE IN FAMILY (AND HOW TO STRENGTHEN YOURS)

When working with my clients, I always communicated to them the value in strengthening their families. It was probably the single biggest differentiator in my arsenal that set my services apart from everyone else's on Wall Street. Together with my clients, I often worked to emphasize the inherent value in each member of their family and to build on that value by creating more.

That practice stayed with me as I retired from my career in finance and opened my boutique consulting firm, MAG7 Consulting. (The full name is actually "Magnificent 7," a reference to the seven lessons you never learn in school.) In my Wall Street days and now, I always remind my clients that they and the members of their family are stronger when united as a team. I've always helped my clients' kids with talking points and tactics that aren't taught in school. I've built a career on investing my time in my clients and their families.

I learned that bringing families together is an incredibly rewarding way to spend your career. I'm curious by nature, and I found it so interesting to get to know families as a unit and as individuals. I knew their names, their birthdays, and key aspects of their family's life.

In fact, a lot of what I did was *strengthen* my clients' families by getting to know them, by taking a deeper dive into what made them tick, made them work. It was helpful for them and thoroughly enjoyable for me.

THE SEVEN LESSONS YOU NEVER LEARNED IN SCHOOL

The seven lessons in this book, which make up chapters 3–9, are what I call the Seven F's: Family, Faith, Friends, Fitness, Financial, Fun, and Filanthropy. Each one is a deeper dive into the principles you need to be successful in life and business—lessons you won't find in a classroom or a textbook. I made it a point to impart these lessons to my clients throughout my career in finance. Not only did they set me apart, but they also helped these families grow.

Throughout my financial career, in fact, much of my narrative could be boiled down into a single, all-encompassing effort: encouraging people to incorporate the principles of the Seven F's into their lives. "No one else will talk about these with you," I would say, "but I'm here to tell you that they are a derivative of your overall plan."

It's one thing to list out the Seven F's and hang them on a wall in your kitchen. But true growth requires more commitment, more practice—something I was all too happy to engage in with my clients. The hard part about these seven principles is learning how to navigate them on a daily basis and to master keeping them in balance through the different seasons of life. For example, there's a period in which a family might be spending 85 percent of their time on financial stewardship, leaving the other 15 percent to be diversified across the other six F's. But most families are amazed at how shifting from giving 2 percent to philanthropy to contributing 5 percent can make a measurable difference in their lives.

Eventually, I turned to authoring family charters for my clients. I'll talk about these charters in more detail in chapter 2, but for now I'll say that the challenge of having a charter is similar to that of the Seven F's: in a word, *execution*. How do we put that charter consistently into practice? How do we keep it from winding up on a bookshelf or in a drawer or filing cabinet? How does it become the beating heart of how a family operates and relates to one another and the world?

My answer to those questions has always been that *I* was to go the extra mile to keep the charter alive. I scheduled executive reviews with families and called them monthly to check in and see how it was going. "Hey, what are you doing for fun?" I would ask them. "Are you traveling? Let's talk about giving. What kind of plan do we have for philanthropy? Are you active on any boards of organizations that are doing things you're excited about?"

The impact those ongoing conversations have had and continue to have is incredible. Through them, I cultivate much deeper relationships with my clients—relationships that go farther than discussing stocks and bonds, or growing a client's money, or projecting what economic changes could result from upcoming elections. All those are important, of course. But there's real and often untapped value in cultivating significant relationships with the people who are your clients.

Those relationships have always been born out of my efforts to be far more interest*ed* than interest*ing*. They have always come from acting on my innate curiosity, asking questions, and learning.

ABOUT THIS BOOK

Winning the Game of Life: The Seven Lessons You Never Learn in School is all about the practical, adaptable strategies that I've developed over my career in finance, working with successful families, and at MAG7 Consulting. They can be used by anyone, at any age or level of education, and in any career.

The strategies I offer you are particularly concerned with family governance and raising world-class young minds. We'll dive deep into the Seven F's that have helped so many families win the game of life, and I'll also offer eighteen tactics to get young minds going in the fast lane. Along the way, you'll discover the value that comes from having—and executing—a family charter and how that charter can help you deliver true legacy to your family. I'll share stories from MAG7 Consulting, and I'll share the secrets of how we've helped successful families build legacies that last.

I'm here to help you elevate the next generations of your family to achieve amazing things and, in the process, to become a better version of yourself.

CHAPTER 1

BEING A VALUE CREATOR

WHEN MY SON and daughter reached driving age, I instructed them in a bit of seemingly unconventional behavior. "When our housekeeper gets here, go get her car keys," I'd say. "Don't even ask—just move her car and wash it."

My kids didn't bat an eye. By that age, they were well-versed in creating value for others. They'd had a lifetime of practice.

Our housekeeper was paid well for her time, of course, but it was important for me to demonstrate our appreciation for her in ways that went beyond compensation. And it was equally important to reinforce in my kids how to create value for others and show them how they could intentionally bring positive experiences into someone else's life.

Before long, taking a visitor's keys, moving their car, and washing it became second nature for my kids. In fact, they started taking *everyone's* keys and washing *everyone's* car. When the person visiting our house wasn't someone they knew well, they would ask permission to move the car. "Hey, Mr. Williams," my son would politely say. "Could I have your keys?"

It was always interesting for me to watch that interaction play out. Sometimes, Mr. Williams would ask why my son wanted his keys.

"So I can give it a nice wash," came the reply.

"For free?"

"Yeah."

Answer me this: who does that for someone?

When was the last time you drove to someone's house, rang the doorbell, and handed over your keys to their kids because they asked if they could wash your car? Unless you've been to my house, I'm going to guess it was…maybe never.

But if you've had that experience, you know it creates immediate, immeasurable value for everyone involved.

It's no secret around my house that creating value by doing something for someone else makes me feel good. I always explain that to the people I work with, too. "You're not doing this for reciprocity," I say. "If you do something for someone else, and you're expecting something in return, you lose. It's just that simple."

Of course, there is clearly reciprocity that happens. There is *science* behind reciprocity. And historically, we've seen groups like those in the eighties—ones that handed out free flowers because they knew it made people far more likely to give a donation in return. In my experience, eight or nine out of ten people reciprocated when I did something nice for them, but that was never the purpose of it.

Creating value is about doing things authentically, for the right reasons. If you do that, you'll become happier. You're going to feel good about doing something nice for someone else.

In the Garapedian family, that's the way we roll.

VALUE CREATION STARTS AT AN EARLY AGE

When we're talking about value creation, there are three types a person can create: material value, emotional value, and spiritual value. Kids aren't going to be generating a lot of material value, but they're excellent at creating emotional and spiritual value by helping someone else.

I know, because I raised my kids to be people who always look for ways they can do exactly that. I always wanted them to be agents of health. That meant I was always a big advocate for rooting for the underdog or finding ways to help someone who was having a hard time.

But what does that look like in day-to-day life? An underdog could be a kid who doesn't fit the "ideal" physical mold and gets made fun of for what they look like. A person having a hard time could just be a kid who's extremely introverted and shy.

We should teach our young people to be value creators at an early age. They don't all have to be washing cars. Any kid from five to fifteen years old can help another kid with an emotional issue they're facing, be a real friend, or stick up for someone who's being bullied. They could help another kid with their homework or even choose them first for a team.

That's something I often encouraged my son and daughter to do. "When you're picking people for teams," I'd say, "I want you to think of someone who is the most likely to get picked last and pick them first."

"Why, Dad?" they'd object. "We want to *win*."

That's understandable. We've all been there, on that schoolyard, when it's time to choose teams for flag football, kickball, or any other team sport. We all know what it's like to want to win.

For a moment, imagine that you're a kid again. You happen to be the absolute worst flag football player at your school, but you're made team captain at recess—and you get to pick your team. Who do you choose first? If you're like most kids, you pick Bobby, the best flag football player, because he'll make up for your lack of skill. That's how the game is won, right? With kids, it's not surprising that there are always a few who get picked last...over and over and over again.

But I taught my son and daughter a different way to win.

"It's not all about winning the game," I told them. "It's about helping other people and demonstrating that you have confidence in them."

And *that* creates value.

Maybe you haven't encountered this idea before, and maybe your kids are older and didn't have childhood to start building a foundation of value creation. That's okay; just start where you are. Kids who are sixteen or older can create value in a different way.

At sixteen, for instance, most kids don't have the money to go out and buy lunches for others. I love doing that as an adult. If I'm ever in a restaurant and see a friend or a client, I pick up their check, and they never know it. That's something a person can do to create material value, but they have to have material means to do it. Kids need other ways to create value—like washing cars.

Or they could deploy one of my eighteen tactics: making reels. You'll find it at the end of this chapter.

CREATING VALUE IS MORE THAN MONETIZING

I'm big on research. A while back, I learned that when a person has a negative episode, they need three positive episodes to break even and five positive episodes to offset the negative one enough that they can thrive.

For me, I've always framed that statistic as an opportunity. "Here's the rule," I say to my family, my co-workers, and even my clients. "To really help someone grow, and to really grow ourselves, we have to play offense with the positive."

I'll say that again: to really, *really* grow, you need positive experiences. Why? Because positive things make you feel good. If you feel good, and happy, you'll be in a mindset to learn, and learning plays an enormous role in personal growth.

Clearly, we'll all have negative experiences; that's just life. Some negatives can be significant, even overwhelming—for instance, if someone you're close to dies. That's heavy. But I learned years ago how critical our mindset is, especially when we experience negative situations. Mindset can make all the difference in the way we process events in our lives.

So, the secret is this: intentionally bring in positive episodes.

That's what being a value creator is all about.

CREATING VALUE THROUGH MINDSET: HELPING SOMEONE FIND THEIR PAIN POINTS AND ALLEVIATE THEIR SUFFERING

Creating value through mindset is best explained by considering how some of the most successful people in the world got there: by helping *others* get where they want to be.

Throughout my career, I made it a point to take an interest in where others wanted to be. That was just part of my mindset and my narrative. Every time I walked into a room, I was already thinking of how I could help the people around me. Remember my four questions? These have always been my North Star: *Where were you before? Where are you now? Where do you want to be? How are you going to get there?*

The result of my style of financial planning was that I spent around 90 percent of my time discussing things with my client that weren't their stock portfolio. We just talked a lot about life.

And those conversations always led me to how I could help.

I made a practice of always doing whatever I could to make someone's life better. Sometimes I helped directly by creating a financial or family plan that put their goals within reach. If I couldn't help a person directly, I made sure to introduce them to someone who could.

This is a lot of what I break down for the young minds I work with as I help them create value through a help-oriented mindset. Who is the person who has just crossed your path? How did they get to where they are? What can you do to help? Like I mentioned before, kids are excellent at helping spiritually and emotionally, so when I work with them, I always make "help" about those aspects.

DOING A "FORMAL DISCOVERY": WHAT'S HURTING? HOW CAN I HELP?

Most times, knowing how to help someone means going deeper and learning where their pain is. I need to know where someone is suffering to know how I can be an agent of help in that area. But here's the real question: *How* do you help a person find their pain points and alleviate their suffering?

It's actually simple (which is not the same as *easy*): just ask them.

Not right out of the gate, of course; you have to warm up the conversation first. And it's also supremely helpful to be interest*ed* instead of interest*ing*, as I mentioned in the introduction to this book, and to make your interactions all about *them*. Questions like, "Mr. Johnson, when you're not being so successful and running your company, tell me—out of curiosity—what do you do for fun?" can be a great place to start. If the hypothetical Mr. Johnson says he likes to play golf, you could then say, "Oh, where are some of the places you like to play?" And so on.

It's also incredibly beneficial to learn how to read body language. For years, I actually paid consultants to educate me on body language to the point that I could x-ray someone's soul just by noting their mannerisms and how they moved. I was able to tell whether someone was comfortable engaging in the conversation at hand, and if they weren't, I was confident that I could help them be comfortable.

As you can imagine, this skill not only helped them; it helped me.

For instance, throughout my career, I found that when a married couple came to my office, the wife often tended to wallflower. That's not helpful for anyone, particularly her, and it can't be much of an enjoyable experience to sit at a table being talked over for several hours. So I made sure to position my own chair at the table in such a way that I could make sure she felt valued enough to take part in the conversation—sometimes to the extent that she could be more than half of the conversation.

For what it's worth, that was another differentiator for me—so many times in my field, the men were arrogant. They didn't give a woman the kind of energy that told her she was important at the table. I wanted every woman who came to my office to know that I respected her intelligence and knowledge.

All that said, helping someone the right way can mean doing a formal discovery. That process usually involved fifty or sixty questions, an hour of conversation, and lots of furious notetaking. (Back in the day, we weren't allowed to record conversations.)

Many times, someone would pause to ask me what, exactly, the purpose of the process was.

"It's a lot like when you go to the doctor," I'd explain. "The nurse is going to ask you all those vital questions about your health. They'll want to know what medicines you're taking, whether you have a family history of cancer, whether you smoke or drink and how often, right?"

"Right."

"Well, I need to know what's hurting you, what your hopes and dreams are, and where you want to be so I can help you get there."

Before I could even consider giving my clients any solutions I needed to know big things—the kind that weren't always easy for them to articulate, like how much risk they could tolerate.

But getting to those important answers often takes smaller, more approachable questions. In the case of risk tolerance, I usually couldn't just out and out ask a person what their risk tolerance was (unless they were a seasoned investor, perhaps, who came to me with an already expertly diversified portfolio that had been making them money for years). It was far more helpful to ask questions like, "Mr. Smith, if you're driving on the freeway, what lane do you drive in?"

"Why do you ask?" he might answer.

"I'm just curious."

"I drive in the middle lane."

"How fast do you go? Over 80 miles per hour?"

"Yes."

By asking these kinds of questions, I could get a much truer sense of Mr. Smith's risk tolerance. Think of it this way—anyone can come in with a canned response, prepared for the moment someone asks them about risk tolerance. That answer may or may not reflect how they truly feel. But knowing that a person drives in the middle lane, over the speed limit, means they're taking more risk on the freeway. More often than not, that comfort with risk-taking translates to their finances.

And I could break that down for Mr. Smith very easily.

"Let's put this in the perspective of your stock portfolio," I could say. "Do you want to take a risk that could cost you a standard deviation of 16 percent—a million dollars if the market went down?"

"There's no way I could handle that."

"Okay, then we shouldn't have you 100 percent in the market. What about if you were to lose 8 percent of your money?"

"I can handle that."

"Okay, that means we need about half of your money in bonds to mitigate risk."

At the end of the day, there are all kinds of ways to get someone to articulate their comfort level with risk, and it's the same with just about any pain point. The thing to remember is that going through a discovery process and drilling down will yield much truer results. In turn, they will help you hone your solutions and create much more value in the process.

One last thing: oftentimes, my discovery process involved drawing a mind map of deliverables, using the client's name as an origin point and branching out with circles and boxes that contained possible deliverables based on the answers to my four guiding questions. The method of discovery isn't as important as finding your way to the answers.

The key is to let those answers inform your plan.

HAVING THE RIGHT FOUNDATION

I'm going to talk about plans a lot in this book because they're just that important. A plan provides a structure, process, and purpose to focus on.

That last one is critical—I always drilled down on finding someone's purpose. I would use the analogy of building a skyscraper, let's say a hundred floors. To build that tall we're going to need a really deep foundation—a mile or more—so that skyscraper is strong enough to stand on its own.

Having a solid financial plan is incredibly important. But so is having a family plan, a meal plan, a plan for health and wellness.

That's another facet of why I attach so much importance to connecting people. Knowing doctors, surgeons, cardiologists, dieticians, state attorneys—you name it—was invaluable. With the "golden rolodex" I built, I could always say to someone, "Oh, you should talk to this guy."

I knew I could build a plan for someone's finances, but I couldn't do it for someone who wanted to overhaul their diet and lose weight. "Get with a dietician," I'd say. "They'll put you on a regimented meal plan, and you'll lose one to two pounds a week. But I'm not a doctor; I'm not going to be able to do that for you."

What I could—and did—say was that it's always worthwhile to spend money on someone who can.

Because the truth is (and I'll talk about this in detail in chapter 10) you also need coaches and mentors. You need an entire team around you for all your different needs, each member of your team crafting a plan according to their expertise.

All those plans will come together to form *the* plan and structure for your life.

IT ALL STARTS WITH RELATIONAL AND TRANSFORMATIVE ENERGY

Throughout my finance career, I never wanted to come off as a salesman. I may have been in an industry where I was paid based on commission, but I did not want to be considered a transactional person.

Although I was clearly in a transactional world, I wanted to be a relational and transformative person. I wanted to give that energy to the families I helped. That meant, as I've said, talking about things that were important, doing the discovery, and learning about their families. From that perspective, any "get this commission" mindset always gave way to "how can I help." I honed my skills as a value creator, and I absolutely fell in love with the process.

Like I said before, I love to show people that the best way they can grow is by helping someone else achieve their dreams and goals. I love to demonstrate that becoming a leader is vital and that the only way to demonstrate leadership is through your actions.

I especially love teaching these principles to young kids. I love to get into leadership discussions with them. I'll talk about the example I gave earlier: choosing the "weak link" first for their flag football team and empowering that kid. It takes leadership born out of relational and transformative energy to do that.

In leadership exercises with kids, I use the word "empower" a lot. I love to empower those kids, to see their faces when they're surprised that I picked so-and-so first for the team—or that they *themselves* were chosen first when they expected to be picked last. Time and time again, I've heard the same question. "Why'd you pick me first?" they ask.

"I love your energy," I'll say, "and I want you in the foxhole with me, buddy."

Can you imagine what that feels like? Go back to your own child-hood—maybe you were the team captain, but maybe you were the kid who got picked last. What if someone had looked you square in the face and said, "I want *you* with me when life get tough"? How might it have impacted your life if someone demonstrated that kind of confidence in you at an early age?

How might you express that kind of confidence in someone and change their life *today*?

TACTICS

At the end of most chapters, I'll go into more detail about a few of my proven tactics for winning the game of life.

TACTIC #1: MAKING REELS

Kids who are between the ages of ten and fifteen are great at this. Anytime you're at a wedding, anniversary, or other significant event, have your kid ask the host or hostess for permission to interview people at the party and get testimonials of guests saying something nice about the host. Then, when they come back with twenty-five video clips, give those clips to a videographer who can transform them into a five-to-seven-minute short movie about the birthday party (or whatever the event was). When I've done this in the past, I've paid a videographer, but regardless, the kid who is conducting the interviews and filming the clips has done the real work of creating value.

This tactic also works for adults. I've personally used it many times—to great success.

CHAPTER 2

CREATING A FAMILY CHARTER AND COAT OF ARMS

LOTS OF FAMILIES have chores, but mine never did. The word "chores" has negative connotations, so we had "gigs." We also never had an "allowance." We were paid for the gigs we took on.

Regardless of my official title, I've always been an entrepreneur, and the entrepreneur in me has always believed in results pay. If one of my kids did something above and beyond their regular household gigs, such as waxing my car after washing it, I would compensate them for the work. My wife and I clearly communicated to our kids the value of family contributions. "You're a part of this family," we said, "and that means there are things you need to do."

"Like what?"

"Well, you need to change the water for the dog. You need to make your bed."

Actions like those are "table stakes." If my kids wanted to be paid for something they did around the house, they had to up the ante and do something that went above and beyond.

My parents laid out similar structures and opportunities for me.

They also made the decision early on to invest in my sister and me by giving us collateral that would serve us well in the future. For starters, my parents did a lot of entertaining. There were always adults around, and I learned at an early age how to carry on conversations with intelligent people.

More than that, even, Mom and Dad paid for lessons—lots and lots of lessons. I started taking professional lessons at a magic shop in Los Angeles when I was really young, learning magic tricks that eventually got me in front of people and taught me showmanship. It was extremely serendipitous—the experience really served me well with public speaking (which is a value add for anyone, in any career).

When we were young, my parents also ingrained in us that we were going to college. Period. My sister achieved a 4.0 GPA to become the valedictorian of her high school and later earned her doctorate at the London School of Economics. I knew which college I wanted to go to by the time I'd reached the ripe old age of six years old. In fact, I vividly remember watching a University of Southern California football game with my dad (who was a proud Ohio State grad) and seeing O. J. Simpson win a Heisman Trophy and the Rose Bowl in 1968. I made my decision that day.

But none of that would have happened if Mom and Dad hadn't had a plan.

WHY A FAMILY CHARTER AND COAT OF ARMS?

Focusing on my clients' families played a huge role in how I differentiated myself in my career. But it was also how I made them feel special and really helped them. Everyone else on Wall Street was doing financial plans; I was the only one doing them in conjunction with a family plan. A lot of families I've seen through the years have their financial plan locked down, but when it comes to their families they just "wing it." Let me tell you—one of the most important decisions you can make as a family is to say, "Hey, let's be intentional about what we do and how we do it. Let's *not* wing it."

"Not winging it" means articulating a plan for your family. In my world at MAG7, it means talking about the Seven Fs, creating a family charter and coat of arms, and digging into what you could do for your family as a whole.

First things first: what do I mean by "family charter" and "coat of arms"?

You can think of a family charter as a kind of constitution specific to your family. And just like our United States Constitution, your family charter outlines the core values and beliefs that make your family what it is. It represents the best of who you are, and who you can be, as individuals who are committed to a shared, family legacy.

A coat of arms, on the other hand, leans into centuries of tradition; it is a visual representation of a family's values and attributes. It's often depicted as a shield decorated with symbolic colors and images and flanked by animals. Each color, image, animal, and word incorporated proclaims the family's values and inner truths.

I always get a lot of enjoyment out of seeing faces light up when people see the family coat of arms we created for them. To see something so personal to them is always deeply meaningful, and I love watching their reactions. I love how the artwork empowers these families to bring structure into their lives. It's rewarding to see the faces of parents who read the family plan my team and I created for them and hear them say, "We are going to be very different when we do these things."

Having a family plan is more than just having ideas written down. It's creating values that become a family's heritage and legacy to be passed down and treasured—just as much or more than financial wealth. I always explain to my clients that if they were to unexpectedly pass away, 90 percent of their money would not make it to the third generation—their grandkids wouldn't benefit from their wealth. But the thing is, it's not *just the money*. It's also their heritage. And if they want either of those to survive beyond their own children's generation, they need a plan.

I can tell you from experience that a family charter that covers the Seven F's will give your family confidence. It will give you structure, process, and a way to win this game of life. It will help each member of your family be the best they can be. It will help you be the best parent you can be.

Don't wing it.

Each family charter and coat of arms we create at MAG 7 is personalized to the family it's being created for. Learning about these families is a version of doing the formal discovery I described in chapter 1. These interviews are extremely vulnerable for everyone involved. We get into sensitive topics—faith, philanthropy, all the topics most families keep close to the chest, but I welcome the vulnerability as a way to forge deep and lasting connections with my clients. Each conversation is a powerful connector between them and me because I really do care about each person. I also have genuine curiosity about how each of the families I work with, most of whom are incredibly affluent, got to where they are.

Of course, it's important to keep these vulnerable conversations as comfortable as possible. Were I to start asking questions like, "Who's the faith leader in your family, and what faith do you follow," the conversation could turn into a metaphorical undressing of the family quickly. I am always professional, but I also make every effort to frame my questions in a whimsical, non-threatening way. Oftentimes, I'll get a call from a family member after our discovery process is over. "You made that so fun," they'll say.

Each time I go through the discovery process, it's very gratifying for me personally. I enjoy learning about how families practice philanthropy, how they practice things like chores with their kids. No two families are the same.

STORYTELLING AS STRATEGY AND LEADERSHIP BY EXAMPLE

When I was a boy, my dad's favorite hobby was woodworking. We had a woodshop in our garage, and I could often be found helping him there. In my earliest years, my job was sanding. That's what I could do, and I was a good sander. I would stand for hours and hours and hours, switching out sandpapers with different grains on them as the task required, the air perfumed with sawdust and resin. Out of those woodshop sessions, Dad and I built a boat together. It was incredible.

Most days, to pass the time while we worked, Dad told stories about what shaped him as a young boy. I'll never forget his telling me about the time he was on a golf course, standing too close to a golfer, and got hit in the temple by the man's club. Hearing him describe the experience, I could smell the grass and hear the club whistling through the air. I could imagine the club's impact as if I had time-traveled somehow, stood in Dad's shoes, and took the hit to my own skull.

Let me tell you—I never forgot that story. Values communicated through stories and by example are the ones that stick. We could've had "don't stand too close to a golfer" scrawled all over the walls of my childhood homes, but the message wouldn't have affected me like Dad's delivery did. I eventually learned to play golf myself, and I never, ever got close enough to another player to be injured by a club.

Dad was also an engineer during World War II. When an enemy blew up a bridge, Dad got called up to reconstruct it. An interesting side effect was that he became very tuned-in to explosives—which translated into my love for fireworks, M-80s, and delayed fuses that would let me plant a firecracker, run two hundred feet back into the family house, and wait for the thrill of the big *pop*. But through my dad's war stories, I also absorbed his anti-gun stance. We never had firearms on our property.

Storytelling taught me so many more values, proverbs, and lessons than I would have learned if I'd encountered them in any other way. Through the years, I've carried the principles with me into my work with clients. I know the kids I work with learn best the same way I did. They will not remember integrity framed on the wall, but they *will* remember a story.

They will also remember action. All those years of sanding at my father's side in our woodshop taught me more than what I learned from his stories. He demonstrated important values—patience, persistence, and doing activities as a family—that I couldn't have learned as deeply or profoundly any other way. In a word, he demonstrated integrity—to the task at hand, and more importantly, as a man, a father, and a friend.

I like to say, "Show me integrity." Show me that when the bill for your meal is wrong, and the error is in your favor, you're going to go out of your way to give an extra tip to your server. That's just one more thing I learned from Dad—he treated restaurant servers with respect and dignity. I watched him learn their names and tip generously. "These folks are making a living," he'd say. "Giving them a higher tip than they expect is an incredible way to demonstrate integrity."

Be like my dad and *demonstrate integrity* to all the people in your life.

FINANCIAL PLANNING VS. FAMILY PLANNING

I've always looked for ways to be a better Barry. A huge part of that was seeing what I could learn from other families. I did a study of some of the most successful families in the country to discover what worked for them. I asked questions, both broad and specific ones. How did all the kids turn out so great? How did they avoid the traps of substance abuse that go hand in hand with affluence? How did the kids know they wanted to go to college and become successful in their own right?

And ultimately, what could I bring back to my own family? How could I make life better for us?

As I discovered things that seemed to work well, for instance, in raising kids or maintaining healthy balances, I collected those best practices and shared them with the clients I knew they could help (without naming names, of course). My track record as a dad and as a man in California with a good marriage (which, unfortunately, is uncommon where I live), gave me credibility. A lot of families lack stability, but I could offer them a different perspective from a truly solid place.

Every family is unique, but there are similarities across successful families. Having family dinners (which I'll talk about in more detail in chapter 3) was one that came up a lot.

I often asked my clients what the most important things were to them. Even now, health and family are always at the top of the list. I'm not a doctor, but I can certainly guide someone toward financial stewardship and family success. I can help you create a plan, a blueprint for your family with guidelines—not rules—for how you want to roll.

Do this in collaboration with your finances, and you'll be in the 1 percent of people who are doing the same.

EXPERIENCING HEALTHY STRUGGLES AND FALLING FORWARD

I had a lifetime of teaching myself to frame "negatives" as positives through playing tennis. I began taking tennis lessons at a young age, and I needed to be able to see losses in a way that would get me back on the court.

In tennis, there's a winner and there's a loser for every match, right? I reframed that. I never thought of it as losing; instead, I taught myself that there's a winner and there's a *learner* in every match. How fun is that? I was always either winning or learning. If I didn't win a match, what did I learn from it?

This "fail forward" mentality was a really important tool because it got me on the tennis court to compete. Learning literally kept me in the game, and I played on both my high school and college teams.

I wasn't given any handouts after college as I built my business from scratch, but the one thing I had was outstanding mentors. Like the coaches, piano teachers, and magic instructors from my youth, my business mentors preached the gospel of repetition. "You have to do the reps and go through the processes to be good," they said.

And they were right.

As I've said, building my business required that I make an enormous number of cold calls. Along the way, I met a really bright fellow. He aced all the industry tests, but he had an aversion to rejection and simply could not make the calls. I realized as a rookie that I had better learn to enjoy cold calling and find a way to make it fun, or I wasn't going to be successful.

So, I chose to think of rejection as a positive. I reshaped my thought process so that rejection equaled success. I might make a hundred calls and hear "no" ninety-nine times; I considered those calls as successful as a single "yes."

Next, I built on that mental acuity to look at the *entire process* of calling differently. I truly believed that each call I made was an opportunity for me to offer help to someone who needed it, and I believed in my ability to create value for others. The result? I didn't experience aversion to calling people and asking them questions. The process still required struggling, but it was a healthy struggle that yielded great results.

AN ODE TO THE DISCIPLINE OF REPETITION

My parents invested in all kinds of professional lessons for my sister and me to give us collateral in this world. From piano to tennis to magic to martial arts (I was a black belt in kung fu san soo), we gained tools that could—and did—take us anywhere. I learned process, discipline, and repetition, all because my mom and dad believed there was material value in having those tools in my personal toolkit.

And to this day, I love discipline. I love practicing something every day. Music, magic, martial arts—these set me up for my life, my career. I arrived on Wall Street leaps and bounds ahead because I had structure and discipline and process. "Show up on time," they said, "and make two hundred phone calls a day."

No problem.

When I played competitive tennis, I enjoyed the practices. I enjoyed the process of working out. I loved doing drills; I still love the protocols of repetition. When I get out on the court today—and I still do—I love challenging myself to see how many times in a row I can keep the ball sailing over the net. Repetition, repetition, repetition. It really gets me going.

Tennis wasn't the only area of my life where I practiced repetition. Being a professional magician means constant repetition—I practiced patterns over and over and over again to help my tricks appear natural when I was doing them onstage in front of people.

But even with repetition, sometimes a trick goes awry. That was always fine with me. Just like in tennis, I made a practice out of failing forward as a magician. Whether I was getting up onstage in front of hundreds of people or fifteen people, I was never afraid of messing up a trick because I knew I would learn from it. Sometimes I blew it, and that made me human.

There's one trick I do that involves a glass of water. I ask for a volunteer from someone in the audience, and I pour the glass of water over their head. The trick is that they stay bone-dry—at least, that's how it's *supposed* to work. It's a pretty high-risk/high-reward situation, and I can certainly remember times when it didn't work—and people *did* get wet.

Without giving away the secret, I can say that some liquids won't work for this trick. But I never would've learned that if I hadn't had the wonderfully embarrassing experience of dumping a glass of liquid over someone's head in a *very* nice restaurant and using *very* many napkins to mop up my mess.

But I'll tell you one thing—thanks to my discipline in failing forward, I never used that particular liquid again.

When I think about it, the discipline that took me through 5:00 a.m. workdays and two hundred daily cold calls probably began even earlier than my lessons. I remember watering lawns in my neighborhood and invoicing my neighbors to be compensated for my work. I was entrepreneurial at a young age and didn't even know it.

And if discipline, structure, and having a plan did all that for me, just imagine what it could do for your family.

Imagine what could happen if your best intentions for your family were written down, mapped out, and made concrete.

Imagine how things could change if you knew, beyond any shadow of doubt, that you'd left a heritage of self-belief in your kids.

The best thing my dad ever did for me, besides loving me unconditionally, was to always let me know that he believed in me. He gave me the gift of self-confidence by demonstrating his belief in me. Whatever belief I have in myself started with him.

Seventy-five percent of winning the game of life is self-belief. We live in the greatest country in the world—a capitalist society in which working hard, demonstrating a solid work ethic, and putting time in can get you far. But these only make up about 25 percent of what it takes to *win*.

From what I've seen, today's young minds only have about 25 percent self-belief. That's staggering, isn't it?

But imagine the world they could create if we could help them raise that percentage to where it should be.

Imagine what they could do if they had a plan.

UP NEXT

The remaining chapters of this book are dedicated to each of my Seven F's. Get ready to take a deeper dive into each one and learn how these tools can help your family win the game of life.

THE SEVEN LESSONS YOU NEVER LEARNED IN SCHOOL

LESSON 1

FAMILY

In the heart of the Garapedian family, the essence of family is "celebrate with the unwavering commitment of joy." Our foundation principles revolve around being present for one another every moment and cherishing the small joys. As we support each other through life's larger challenges, we cultivate an environment where laughter is abundant. Frequent big hugs and declarations of love are our daily melody. Sunday dinners are cherished as a tradition symbolized by our open door, extending a warm invitation to family and friends alike, reinforcing our belief and strength of community and the value of face-to-face connections as mentors and advocates for everyone else, others, and our family. We strive to embody the best version of ourselves, teaching and learning the virtues of humility and hard work.

—excerpted from the Garapedian family charter

WELCOME TO THE first F: Family.

Simply put, Family is everything. At MAG7 Consulting, we put a lot of energy into strengthening families and strategizing healthy family dynamics. It's very real. Not everyone has a family in the traditional sense—some people are single and have lots of friends, their chosen family, but that doesn't mean family is any less powerful to them. In fact, family is often the single biggest motivator (behind personal health) for almost everyone I've encountered in my life. That's true for business professionals as well as parents of uber-successful families. Family is at the heart of every decision, strategy, and purpose.

I welcome you to think through the elements of the paragraph at the beginning of this chapter and consider which of them could benefit your family. You can also consider the following principles, which are the bread and butter of our family dynamic:

Family members are always there for each other—not only for big life crises, but for the little things like driving each other to and from the airport. The drive time is a chance to be together with no distractions.

Laugh out loud, hug often, and tell each other you love them a lot. (Yes, that is actually written into our charter.)

Sunday dinners are a must, and during dinner, we always put our technology away. All family members and extended family—including kids and close friends—always have a seat at the table. (In our world, everyone knows the Garapedian family has an open-door policy for Sunday dinner, and they're welcome. Last-minute? No problem. Have an issue? Bring it. We are here for you.)

Make life better for your kids by being the best version of yourself. Teach your kids the value of money. Instill values of work ethic. (Do all this, and no one in your family will have an attitude of entitlement. Our kids certainly don't.)

The balance between work and family is paramount. Never miss a birthday party, a graduation, or a school or sporting event. (Let me tell you, this one is powerful. Garapedians do not miss each other's events. We go to sporting events, school events, birthday celebrations—there's good collateral to be had in showing up for each other.)

For the most part, our family keeps to these principles. We spend time together and spread optimism. We believe in each other, instill confidence in each other, and advocate for one another.

We are here for each other no matter what.

From talking on the phone to attending events to family dinner, it's been that way for years.

GROWING UP GARAPEDIAN

As is the case for most of us, the baseline of what I know about family comes from my personal experience. I was fortunate to grow up Garapedian, in a family that prioritized personal development, service to others, and togetherness.

My dad was a professor of journalism. The boat we built together in his woodshop was a sailboat, and when it was finished, we learned to sail it together. But what I remember about the experience is less about sand and sea and more about water and wood. I'll never forget all the hours I spent watching him curve a straight plank by submerging it in water, bending it, letting it dry. He also mastered the art of lamination, and I like to think we were both specialists in that area. Under his guidance and example, I excelled in laminating different types of wood together to make breadboards. We made many and gave them as gifts.

The lessons I learned from my father went beyond the woodshop, of course. One of the lessons was consistency in practice. I remember hitting tennis balls against our garage door, practicing night after night. Any chance I got, I would put all those tennis balls in a basket, balance them on my bicycle, and ride to the local park. I made a bee-line for the tennis courts, hoping for pickup games with other players.

We did not have gardeners when I was growing up. Every weekend, my sister and I did yard work with my father. He would start the lawnmower when I was too young to do that part myself, and then he would edge around the lawn while I mowed. As I mentioned in chapter 2, we never got an allowance for those responsibilities because Mom and Dad believed helping with yard work, cleaning my room, and making my bed were the table stakes of being part of our family. They weren't about money. They were what we did for each other and did together.

Outside of table stakes, family dinners were a huge part of life. I come from a big Armenian family, so you could say those dinners were also part of our cultural heritage, just like the vacations we took together and the way we took time to entertain each other. I was always playing piano in front of my family, always doing magic, always staging talent shows with my cousins.

When I was a young boy, I was always excited for these gatherings. *I'm going to do a magic trick*, I would think. *I can't wait.* That collection of memories, along with the ones I have of being in front of people and playing piano, beginning at age eight or nine, is fantastic. As you might imagine, I was never nervous in front of people. That's also thanks to my parents, who enrolled me in lessons and gave me the opportunity to gain practical experience at such an early age. So much about those experiences translated into who I am today and how I live my life.

They still resonate.

I can still hear the swish of sandpaper over pine, still smell the perfume of freshly cut grass, still feel the *thwack* of a tennis ball reverberating through the air. And when I remember, I think of all I learned as a Garapedian: patience, work ethic, and the value of being part of a family that operates as a team.

Family is a conduit. What's transmitted by and through your family is up to you.

BRINGING A POSITIVE MINDSET

One of the most impactful ways your family dynamic shapes individual family members is by laying the foundations for mindset. If tended correctly, this can be an amazing opportunity. I learned early in life that a positive mindset is all about preparation, proper technique, helping others, and being a giver.

PREPARATION

My father taught me the six P's: preparation and prior planning prevents poor performance—meaning, you always have to be prepared.

In my house, preparation means early to bed. It means always looking for a better way to do things. It means looking at the good in everything, which I did from an early age. I've never been a negative person, and, generally speaking, I trusted everyone I met. It has served me well—partially through the law of attraction, which I'll discuss in more detail in chapter 4.

PROPER TECHNIQUE

Consider this: if you're playing tennis, you want to learn the proper techniques like grips and footwork early on. It's the same for swimming—when you watch a swimmer, you can tell when they have the techniques down.

My parents taught me that a positive mindset also means equipping yourself with the best techniques possible; we aren't born knowing how to do everything. Mom and Dad knew that, so they found experts to train my sister and me. Throughout my life, I always had great coaches, mentors, and teachers. Learning from others began with tennis, piano, and magic lessons, some of which began when I was only seven years old.

And it didn't stop there.

By the time I reached adulthood, I had learned well what my parents knew all along: paying for mentorship and coaching was an investment in my future. I accordingly spent thousands of dollars on my own personal consulting and mentorship from individuals at the top of their field. I wanted to learn from the best in the world. And, thanks to Mom and Dad, I knew that getting the right people around me meant I would learn the proper techniques for the task at hand.

Ask anyone, and they'll tell you I'm really into technique. Knowing I have the right ones to achieve my goals efficiently and to the best of my ability fortifies my positive mindset.

HELPING OTHERS AND BEING A GIVER

You know by now that my mindset is always fixed on trying to help other people. I do it because it creates value for them by adding to something they're already doing. I also do it because adding value to someone else's efforts makes me happy. Creating value for someone else gives me joy.

The popular mindset will tell you otherwise. It will whisper, yell, and scream to you that getting something you want requires *taking* it from situations, people, or circumstances.

I simply don't operate that way.

Ever since I was young, "people are taking advantage of you" has been a common refrain in my life. But giving has always been authentic for me, and it has always been how I connected with people.

Suffice it to say that I am not a taker. I am a giver, to the extent that sometimes my wife has chimed in with everyone else to say, "You're giving so much that you don't get back. You are letting people take advantage of you."

She isn't wrong, but here's the thing—*I have always been okay with that.*

Maybe that's a radical way of thinking, but it's true. I know people take advantage of me from time to time, but what I get from giving to them makes it okay.

CONNECTING TO THE MOMENT

Let me tell you about weddings. I've been to hundreds of them, so I can say with a fair amount of confidence that the best part isn't the food, or the DJ, or the first moment when everyone gets up and starts dancing before their drinks have kicked in. The best part of any wedding is the end—when everyone is having fun.

At a recent wedding, I had a goal: to connect to the moment, capture that fun, and give it as a gift. I decided to deploy Tactic #1 and create a reel.

That night, I waited for the fun to emerge. Sure enough, there was a moment when everything clicked, and people went cuckoo. The dance floor was packed; everyone was screaming and yelling, "Three, two, one!"—a countdown for something I never quite figured out, because I was absorbed in the happiness and joy written across the faces around me. Everyone was drinking, of course, but the point was that they were having fun.

I seized the moment, went out on the dance floor, and started videoing. I had already decided I would talk to a hundred wedding guests, so I began circulating with my phone. I asked people to tell me something great about their group. I asked them what the bride and groom meant to them.

It was a blast.

I stayed at the wedding until they turned off the music around 11:30 that night, and my clients got to see me hanging in there with them. They saw me fly out on a red-eye and get home early the next morning, all to celebrate an important moment with their family.

That's volume. That's being connected. That is creating value and seeing it through by showing up. Most importantly, it's part of making everyone's experience better.

When it was all said and done, I took the footage to my videographer and had it edited down into an eight or ten-minute reel, which

I gave to the bride and her parents—clients of mine who weren't out there getting sweaty with the crowd. That way, they were still able to experience it.

TACTICS

TACTIC #2: DASH DINNER: CREATING THE MOST MEMORABLE DINNER EVER

Garapedian family dinners are often what I call Dash Dinners.

I gather everyone—somewhere in the neighborhood of fourteen people—around one big table. Then I pose the "table question"—a question meant for everyone at the table to answer.

Let me set it up for you. Once everyone is seated, I call them to attention.

"A wise man once said the most important carving on your tombstone is the dash. It's the line that separates the dates of your birth and your death, and it represents your life. How well do you want to live your dash?"

I then instruct everyone to lift their plates, take the card I hid there in advance, and write down something they want to do before they leave this planet.

Typically, everyone begins feverishly writing. When they're done, I go around and collect the cards in random fashion. I mix them up in a wine decanter and bring them back to the table, where everyone draws a card. When all the cards have been distributed, I begin asking my family members, one at a time, to read them.

In a recent dinner, one of my family members read out, "I want to sing like Whitney Houston for three hours." The table then had three guesses to figure out who authored that card. If no one guesses correctly, there's a reveal. "Barbara," we'll ask, "tell us why you want to sing like Whitney Houston," and she'll tell us about her act.

Learning the *why* behind someone's answer is even more important than the answer itself.

We do this frequently at our family dinners, often to a chorus of *whoa, never seen that before* from newcomers. To mix it up, I often let different family members come up with the questions in advance. A few months before I began working on this book, one of the girls in our family (she was five years old at the time) asked everyone to write down their favorite Disney character.

It was fantastic. A card that read, "Cinderella," was met with shouts of "It's you, it's you!" ringing out across the room. When we finally figured out who chose Cinderella, we asked why. The answer?

"'Cause at home, it's me and the broom," the author said.

Family Dash Dinners begin with questions and guessing, followed by three parlor games. I do ten trivia questions, ten "name that tune" questions with my iPhone hooked up to a Bluetooth speaker, and then ten questions about people in the news. The stakes are high for these parlor games because there's a five- or ten-dollar bill on each question. Without fail, those stacks of money bring a lot of excitement. People get *very* competitive, and it's dead serious. Afterwards, we do twenty minutes of close-up magic.

Dash Dinners easily transfer to different groups outside of the family. I've done them for businesspeople in private dining rooms, for clients in very nice restaurants, and with individuals who are centers of influence in their field; I've even mixed clients and prospects with unbelievable results. Everyone likes to have fun, and we never talk about business. It's all about creating a moment.

As a final touch, I always send out handwritten notes in the days following the dinners. I write about the passions everyone opened up about. If someone spoke about climbing Mount Everest without oxygen, I would write his note about that dream, often sending with it a book on the topic or a non-business book I like. It's a powerful way to make someone feel seen, heard, and remembered.

TACTIC #3: STAY ACTIVELY ENGAGED

I love learning, and I like to attend functions where I have the opportunity to take in new information, wisdom—anything that could help me become a better Barry. When I attend these functions, such as a recent genius network session of the state entrepreneurial group, I'm a very quiet audience member. A lot of people like to raise their hands, ask questions, find some way to toot their own horn. Not me. I just like to sit, listen, and take notes.

When I go to these gigs, I take my Sharpies. I have eight colors. I take notes and write down everything I hear that could add value to me. I color code names, wisdom, strategies. Sure, I could go back and watch the sessions; they're always recorded. But writing ideas down by hand and color-coding what I've learned keeps me actively engaged in the moment. What I write, I remember. It's just part of how I roll and how I think.

Inevitably, these notes inform who I become and how I deploy strategies to help others.

LESSON 2

FAITH

*In the Garapedian family, faith acts as the cornerstone,
guiding our thoughts, actions, and interactions with the
world around us, rooted deeply in Christian values under
the gentle leadership of our matriarch. We are taught not
only to believe in God, but also to cultivate a profound
and personal relationship. We gather around the dinner
table each night to share grace as a cherished tradition.
Pastor Sharon's father reminds us of our spiritual heritage
and the appreciation of our blessing. Our faith is a source
of renewal, driving us to give generously and serve others,
which replenishes our spirit and reinforces our commitment
to a purpose-driven life.*

—excerpted from the Garapedian family charter

THE SECOND F is Faith.

Faith is critical to a healthy family structure, and identifying your family's faith leader is equally important. In our house, my wife, Sharon, is raising our kids on a foundation of faith in God—a foundation that's paired with relationship. She encourages the members of our family to have a very present relationship with God.

Sharon and I trade off on the different leadership areas in our house, and in faith, she is the teacher; I am the learner. Sharon was very clearly the right choice to be our family's faith leader. I went to Sunday school my whole life, but she's even more knowledgeable than I am.

Here are a few of the principles of faith we uphold in the Garapedian house:

Understand that you shouldn't pray for an outcome, but pray for God's will.

In our family, the greatest gift we can give is to pay it forward. Our family rejuvenates itself by helping other people. (This provides our family with a big narrative oriented around action and rooted in today.)

Our family shares grace. (Before every dinner, Sharon's father had a prayer, and it went like this: "Heavenly Father, thank you for this and all our blessings. Amen." We adopted his prayer, and we always start with it. We're not long-prayer people.)

Remain humble. Believe in something greater than yourself. Understand you can only control what's within your power, but God can move mountains.

We are humble people. Everything is purposeful. We believe everything happens for a reason. Our responsibility is to uncover these reasons, learn from them, and lead a meaningful life.

The Garapedian family steps into the future. We continue to honor and expand upon the spiritual legacy invested in us. We ensure that each generation, which is our grandkids, embraces our faith practices to meet the challenges and opportunities of our time by maintaining a close and active relationship with God and instilling these values in our children. We aim to forge a future where the Garapedian family continues to exemplify faith in inspiring both our future generations to lead lives of meaningful impact in enduring phases.

Faith is not only foundational to how we live our lives today, but it also plays a major role in ensuring our legacy of values, heritage, inner truths, and purpose passes to future generations of our family. We choose to pass these values of faith on to our grandkids, and we are intentional and purposeful in that choice. Why? We want to make sure our branch of the Garapedian family tree doesn't wind up like the statistic I quoted earlier in this book.

For us, faith is intrinsic to heritage. It helps us avoid becoming part of the 90 percent of families whose values are lost by the third generation.

SPIRITUAL VS. RELIGIOUS: CREATING VALUE FIRST

Roughly one-fifth of the United States is agnostic, or not religious. I think it's important to note that fact and clarify what I mean (and what I don't) when I use the word *faith*. Specifically, *faith* doesn't have to be about *religion*. I ascribe to Christian faith and values, but I don't read the Bible, and I do not consider myself to be religious. My kids attended Christian universities and retain the values of Christianity.

In the Garapedian family, we also believe in what I think of as the universe. (For what it's worth, I am personally more spiritual, but my family is faith-based.) We believe in the law of attraction—that whatever you put into the universe is what you're going to get.

The law of attraction says that if you think of something, you can make it happen. I can look back across my life and see the evidence of that truth as it played out time and time again. I'm being realistic here, not talking about so-called "woo-woo" things. Put positivity, value, and selflessness into the world, and those gifts will come back to you.

When we talk about creating value through faith, that value comes from living our lives *selflessly*. In my family, we love others, and we connect to something greater than ourselves. Our practice of faith includes acts of kindness, acts of service, praying for others, connecting to God, sharing God's love, and creating a higher mission for life.

Basically, our faith principles form the infrastructure of giving instead of taking. (Let's face it—the world is full of givers and takers. You're either one or the other.) Through our thoughts and actions, each of us chooses whether we give or take. If you choose to be a giver, you can go one step farther and create value by helping someone.

There is immense value in rooting for people and believing in them. Having that mindset makes me authentic with the people in my life, and it means I can cut right through the chitchat.

Look—I don't want to talk about baseball or how it's another beautiful day in Southern California. What I really want is to know about *you*. What can I do to help you? Tell me about your story. What do you do in the morning? What do you do for fun? Maybe you've had career successes; maybe you haven't. All right. But tell me about your family. Tell me about your kids. What are their names?

In those moments, I've learned to be quiet and allow the moment to become all about the other person in the conversation. I don't talk frequently. I don't need to toot my own horn. Instead I choose to give, help, and be quiet, in service to their needs.

That's how I lead.

BRINGING FAITH THAT IS NON-JUDGMENTAL AND GLASS HALF-FULL

Generally speaking, perceptions of faith can be...less than favorable. It's possible that you're reading these words and feel something similar. I can't blame you for those feelings any more than I can deny that a historical precedent for using "religion" as a measuring stick—a way to judge others and find them wanting—has existed for centuries.

But I always impress upon my clients and anyone else who crosses my path that although I choose to live my life according to the principles of Christianity, that doesn't mean I love people of other faiths any less. I appreciate diversity, and that means I don't judge people of other faiths, political convictions, or what have you. Instead, I applaud and love that they have passions.

"Personally, I'm in the middle," I might say when discussing religion or politics, "but I do love your passion." That can be a great way to talk about differing beliefs and acknowledge something that is critically important to someone else without triggering a polarized or confrontational exchange.

Consider this: one precedent does not ensure future certainty. It is entirely possible to build a faith practice around the values of religion that help you uplift, serve, and enhance the lives of others.

I know because I've done it.

And I can tell you that the value of faith directly correlates with the degree to which we reserve our judgment and are intentionally glass half-full with the people we serve.

Simple as that.

TACTICS: FAITH-BASED VALUE CREATION IN ACTION

All right, we now have some great guiding principles of Faith—you can call everything in this chapter thus far *faith in the abstract*. But what does selfless, giving, non-judgmental, glass-half-full faith look like in action?

In this section, I'll offer some strategies that demonstrate how our principles of faith can translate into value creation for clients, family members, or anyone else who comes into your life. Use them in your own family or business or take them as a starting point to develop some of your own.

TACTIC #4: NOTHING HAPPENS UNTIL AFTER YOU COMMIT

As I've said, true value comes when you can help solve a problem or pain point for another person. Discover their pain points by talking to them when things aren't great for them. If you talk to people when life isn't going well—and when you really, truly want to seek out their pain points—they will generally tell you what's wrong. When I've asked, I've heard everything in the book. *Everything.*

Each time, listening to someone gives me the opportunity to step up.

My work with MAG7 often puts me in contact with parents whose kids are making choices that will negatively impact their future. In such a situation, I can leverage my success to gain credibility with a kid who doesn't want to listen to what Mom and Dad have to say. "Hey," I'll say, "let me talk to your son. Let me show him a perspective that's different from yours."

Most of the time, my intervention begins by presenting that kid with a choice.

"You're doing great at this, this, and this," I'll say, "but we need to get back on track in *xyz* area. You have to decide: do you want to do that? Let's start there." If the kid says "yes," we can work on a plan for how we're going to get there.

But first, I ask them to demonstrate, for one week, that they're committed to their decision.

"Show me you're committed," I say, "and I'll help you."

Creating a scenario in which the kid in question must *qualify* for my help is extremely effective. In a typical week-long commitment, I use a kind of disclaimer that outlines what they need to do to earn my help. One way I do this is with a daily, early-morning phone call. "Call me at 7:00 a.m. every day for seven days," I'll say. "If you call me at 7:02, I'm not going to help you. Call me at 7:00 exactly. I'm going to give you something that will absolutely change your life, but you have to qualify."

Whether or not the kid follows through tells me how serious they are about making a change. But it isn't only about meeting that bar. It's also about expressing my *personal* faith in these kids and their potential.

"By the way," I'll say, "your dad isn't giving me any money for this. I'm doing it because I believe in you. I know you're better than what you've been. You just need to demonstrate that for me. So I want you to know that if my phone rolls over to 7:01, you've given up the opportunity for my help. That's okay; you're not ready. I still believe in you. You're just not ready."

Let me tell you—it works.

Why? Because we cut through all the bullshit. "Let's get one thing right—you are better than this," I'll say. "If you want to run around with that 'cool' crowd that's drinking, smoking, and doing all the naughty things, it might be cute right now, but it won't be later on."

TACTIC #5: STORYTELLING AS STRATEGY

To strengthen my point when working with kids, it can be helpful to deploy Tactic #5: Storytelling as Strategy.

In my experience, this has been especially helpful when working with kids who are abusing substances. When the moment is right, I share stories about my fraternity brothers.

In my college years, it was cute to be a big drinker. But a year or two out of college, a large majority of my brothers started calling me and asking for money. "Sam," I'd say, "I love you, but I am fully invested in my securities. I don't have the liquidity to give you what you need. I can't break my stock to give you $5,000. What I *can* give you is thoughts and some help—but if you have a drinking problem, you're talking to the wrong guy. I don't know how to help you with drinking. I don't know how to help you with smoking cigarettes or doing cocaine or any of that naughty stuff. I am not qualified to help you; you need to get the help of a professional."

That story, when strategically applied to the moment, can teach a kid much more than parental discipline ever will—just like my dad's story about taking a golf club to the temple taught me to keep back from the tee box.

Think through your own experiences. How can you use them to strategically transmit wisdom to someone who desperately needs to hear it?

TACTIC #6: BUILD A GOLDEN ROLODEX

I can't overstate the fact that *people need help.* That's just the whole of it. We all need help in some way, shape, or form, and providing that help is how I create value for others. By learning the areas in which people need assistance, I can build a bridge to a helper through a connection.

Building bridges is about building *contacts.*

When I told my fraternity brothers that I couldn't help them overcome issues with booze or drugs, I was speaking from a place of experience. Because believe me, I'd tried to help people with all that stuff. I rah-rahed them and encouraged them the best I could, but I was very disappointed in myself when none of it worked.

All the encouragement in the world won't stop someone from binge drinking when they're addicted to alcohol. I learned well that I can't do everything, but I can help by delegating those jobs to professionals.

Enter the Golden Rolodex.

For those who weren't in business in the 1980s, a Rolodex is a wheel of alphabetized cards containing the numbers and addresses of all the people one needed to keep track of. Sometimes they were encased in plastic, other times brass. The idea was that you could *roll* the Rolodex to find the contact you needed.

"Golden Rolodex" is how I refer to my collection of incredible—and therefore "golden"—contacts (which I also mentioned in chapter 2). These contacts help me be in service to others and address any pain points I've identified but I'm professionally unqualified to address.

There are lots of people in my world—in that Golden Rolodex—that I can refer to someone who needs help. You have an issue with chronic pain? I can connect you with a pain specialist, and if that specialist is booked for the next six months, I can help connect you to someone who isn't. You're trying to lose weight and become fit? I can introduce you to some of the best dieticians and trainers in the nation—people who will help you control your appetite, edit the naughty things like excessive sugar from your diet, and get on a fitness plan that works.

Who do you know that could help someone else? How could you create value for another person by connecting them?

LESSON 3

FRIENDS

In the Garapedian family, friendships are viewed as a mirror of our own values and aspirations, guiding us to associate with individuals who enhance our lives and deepen our understanding of the world. We place great importance on the quality of our associations, believing that the character and the spirit of those we choose as friends contribute significantly to our own personal development. As natural leaders within our circles, we proactively nurture relationships that are grounded in mutual support, understanding transformation is the goal (rather than mere transactions).

As we look forward, the Garapedian family remains committed to cultivating and sustaining friendships that resonate with our core values of leadership, empathy, and authenticity. Our proactive approach to friendship ensures that we not only maintain but actively enrich those relationships, fostering a supportive network that extends beyond mere companionship to form a community of mutual uplifting. By upholding these principles, we aim to ensure that

*what we forge today will grow stronger, offering comfort,
joy, and an unwavering support to future generations of
the Garapedian family, and reinforcing our belief in the
transformative power of genuine connection.*
　　　　　—excerpted from the Garapedian family charter

ON TO THE third F: Friends.

Let's kick off this chapter with a question. Who would you really pick up the phone for?

I'm blessed to have many people in my life that fit into that category. My family, of course, but also—importantly—my friends.

My personal friend groups are broken down into subgroups by commonality or shared common traits. I have many different friends through skiing, tennis, magic, etc. We relate to each other through shared interests, and those interests provide a platform upon which the relational aspects of our friendship can develop. As stated in our family charter, I look at friends as people who help me grow—people I can uplift and who also uplift me. What does that friend look like? Simply someone who is always there for me and makes me a better person—a better version of myself for my friends.

That's incredibly important for all the members of our household. Garapedians want to be around folks that uplift us and make us better, and we want to do the same for the people we call friends. Think of the adage "iron sharpens iron," but consider it in terms of an organic, mutual betterment and growth. Friends exist in a transformative space in our lives, not a transactional one. We're better as individuals because we've chosen to be better together.

Here are a few of the principles of friends upheld in the Garapedian house:

We choose our friends carefully. We are the aggregate of the five people we most associate ourselves with. Remove yourself from pools of pessimism. (We really don't have folks in our lives that are negative nellies or always seem to have a cloud over their head.)

Our family members are leaders in friendship groups, not hesitating to reach out first and step up for a friend in need. (We're always helping people, whether it's emotionally or even financially.)

Our friendships are relational and transformative, not transactional. Our friends will drop everything if need warrants.

Our friends are as easy to be around as we are.

When it comes to friends, I always look to provide them with comfort, safety, and joy in the relationship. To do that requires being incredibly present with the person that's in front of me (or on the phone, or on Zoom, or whatever the case may be). When I'm present with them, I'm not multitasking on my computer or phone or anything else.

Many people I've met believe in the Golden Rule: *Treat others the way you want to be treated.* I have a better rule—what I call the Platinum Rule. It goes like this: *Treat others how* they *want to be treated.*

The Golden Rule is about you.

The Platinum Rule?

It's about *them.*

CARPE THE EXPERIENCE, CREATE RELATIONAL VALUE

In August 2023, I set out on a mountain bike trail with six of my friends. These individuals are all part of the subset of my friend groups that enjoy cycling and have an affinity for long treks through the wilderness.

Which was important because we weren't mounting just any old trail—we had set our sights on the Aquarius Trail in Utah. For the uninitiated, to trek over the Aquarius Trail is to undertake a journey of 200 miles, one-way, over an elevation of 17,000 feet of uphill terrain.

It involves camping, carrying provisions, exposure to the elements—all things that can make or break a friend group.

For my friends and me, the camaraderie, the opportunity to be out in nature while biking through snow and heat, the experience of being hundreds of miles away from any roads…all of it was extraordinarily memorable. Our experience strengthened our friendships and lifted us up. You can't come away from something like that without being changed by it, and we all experienced transformation.

But I'll be the first to tell you that you don't need to spend a week biking through the wilderness of Utah to experience growth and transformation with a friend. You can have—and provide—a transformative experience in a matter of minutes.

I do a lot of gatherings with mastermind groups all over the country, and one of my favorite things to do on these trips—when I land in a ski area, that is—is to focus on the conversations I have while riding a chairlift up the slopes.

Chairlift conversations are like no other conversations. When you're eight, nine, ten thousand feet in altitude, sitting on a chairlift with another person, heading for another run…those conversations are amazingly authentic and real. You're cold, you're eating an energy bar, and you're in the most beautiful place in the world. Be fully present with your conditions and your chairlift companion, and see how much relational value comes of it. It's a perfect setup for open conversation, vulnerability, wonder, and bonding.

Perhaps I'm riding the chairlift with a longtime friend or family member, and in those few minutes our relationships are reaffirmed and strengthened. Or maybe I'm riding with a fellow masterminder—someone I don't know well, but for whom I would like to create value. I assure you there's no better opening to create value for someone than those few minutes of swaying over a backdrop of peaks and pines, snow and sky.

Seize it.

DEALING WITH SOCIAL AWKWARDNESS

Consider this: being suspended over a mountain with a stranger could be someone else's nightmare. Maybe it's *your* nightmare—the same kind of nightmare that relegates you to wallflowering at events. If I was your chair companion, I would intuit that about you right away.

In fact, I make a point to look for social awkwardness so I can create value for the person experiencing it by making them feel more comfortable. It could be that they are extremely introverted, or shy, and I will see an opportunity to bring them into the group by starting a conversation about their hobbies, what they do, where they like to travel—anything that's about them. I'm very tuned into looking for the person who might feel extremely out of place, and I can—and do—soften that feeling by coming to their aid.

In other words, I do what I can to be a friend to that person. If that feels out of your personal comfort zone, remember to do what I do and be more interest*ed* than interest*ing*.

When it comes to speaking with clients, I intentionally get them talking about themselves so that they can relax and feel comfortable. Making the conversation about them allows them to open up. That seemingly small act brings immense value for them because they feel happier and willing to talk about their passions and families, their hopes and fears.

It's also brought huge value to my career.

Getting people to open up is a connection strategy: when people feel comfortable talking to you, you can get a solid grasp on their pain points and how you can help. I consider myself an expert at approaching these conversations and discoveries with a balance of professionalism and childlike wonder. I can talk with people about the things they don't really want to talk about with anyone else, and I can help them have fun in the process. With me, they can let their hair down a little and find the beauty in the moment. They can be present and just have more fun.

When it comes to fun, I always go back to the idea of kids. Why? Because a lot of adults are *just like them*. They want to have fun, and that doesn't change just because they're older. They share that quality with kids and—just like those same kids—having fun is one of the two ways they learn.

I understand that on a foundational level. From my Dash Dinners to storytelling to jumping into the middle of a wedding reception dance floor, I lean into having good, even childish fun. Sometimes my daughter and other family members even have to remind me not to be *too* childish. *All right, fair*, I think, and I rein it in just enough. But I never stop having fun—to the extent that I've made it one of the Seven F's (which I'll talk about in more detail in chapter 8).

The other way adults learn is through real-life experiences. I would go so far as to say that's part of what happens when we trek through the wilderness or sit on chairlifts with others. Through those real-life experiences, we're learning our friendships moment by moment—and experiencing the value of those bonds in the process.

LEARNING THE ART OF COMMUNICATION

My parents taught me tactics and strategies for communication very early in my life. If we were standing in line somewhere, I would watch my father start a conversation with someone. He was almost always the first person to initiate an interaction, usually by looking at something a person was buying or doing. He didn't force the conversation, just let it naturally develop and flow.

Communication is the *art* of making interaction very natural, making it easy, making it fun.

One way to achieve these results is by always looking to learn something about someone. I'm constantly looking forward to growing into the next version of myself. I feel I can learn from others because I was taught so by my mom and dad. "Tell me about your experience of *xyz*," I might begin, and off we go. Before long, I've followed that conversational path into a place of making connections and uncovering all the deep stuff that people don't lead with or even talk about.

That's possible through open communication and connection built on trust.

Which is the whole thing in business, right? You can't do *anything* with your clients unless they feel comfortable with you. Getting to that point means you have to start by building a rapport sturdy enough to *become* trust.

Our whole business was trust. Specifically, we mitigated the two biggest stresses of the financial world: fear and confusion. My strategy was always to break down fear by having transparency and clarity—and to have those, I had to personally open up and be vulnerable.

Expressing my own vulnerability demonstrated my personal willingness to let down my guard and take risks. Showing my clients that I'm human allowed my prospective clients to feel more comfortable and helped them move forward with me.

Trust built on vulnerability is immensely valuable, but I also make a point of connecting with others through generosity. I look to offer value in any way I can, and I demonstrate that value by offering it for free. Remember, there are three ways we demonstrate value: materially, emotionally, and spiritually. Emotional and spiritual value don't cost anything, and most of the time I can give that value by making an introduction for someone.

Sometimes the best way to connect with someone is by giving them a story, which is what I did during the wedding I described in chapter 4. Not only did I connect with all the wedding guests I interviewed, but I also gave the gift of a specific story—the narrative of celebration and joy that was happening on the dance floor that night—to the bride and her family. Connection through story is incredible because it continues to create more opportunities to connect.

TACTICS

TACTIC #7: HANDWRITTEN NOTES

I started creating elaborate, handwritten notes for my clints and associates a long time ago. To this day, I keep seven or eight different personal stationeries and note cards on hand for this purpose. When I meet someone and have a conversation with them, I often send them a personalized note afterward, in which I reference something specific about our interaction.

After playing a round of golf with someone, I might send a note that says, "Bill, it was great seeing you. I'll never forget your second shot on the eighth hole and the way it landed thirty-six inches from the pin. That was a phenomenal shot—I'll always remember it. Loved connecting again. All the best, Barry."

I like to add flourishes to my handwritten notes too—added details that demonstrate the care, thought, and time I've invested while preparing them. (For the record, that's not about me; it's about showing the recipient they are worthy of that kind of investment.) I've mastered the art of melting and dripping wax for use with a personalized seal, which gets pressed into the melted wax and leaves an embossed design with my initial on the outside of the envelope. Sometimes I'll even marble two wax colors together. On the front of the envelope, I use custom return labels from my collection. I have six or seven of them with different themes: golf, ski, a Betsy Ross American flag, tennis racquets...all with my last name and return address. I add enough old-fashioned stamps to cover postage, and that's that.

If you've ever received one of these notes from me, you know right away that they're different. They stand out from every other piece of mail you get. I will tell you from experience, 100 percent of people open them. In fact, the majority of the time, people will take a picture of their note and send it to me. I love those reactions. And I love knowing that when the recipient opens one, they find that the note is about them. It's just one more way to connect, one more way to create value for someone else.

Creating these notes is an active meditation. I write ten of them each week, and it makes me feel good to have that kind of meditative moment built into my process.

LESSON 4

FITNESS

In the Garapedian family, fitness stands as a central pillar, embodying a philosophy of strength, resilience, and leadership. Whether through early-morning swims or reflective meditation sessions, each family member contributes to a culture of continuous self-improvement and accountability. We strive to mirror our own personal philosophies of integrity, compassion, and commitment in each sport or activity we choose and do so with a thorough competitive vision of excellence. Through this integrated approach, we encourage each other to achieve health and well-being in all facets of life.

—excerpted from the Garapedian family charter

THE FOURTH F is Fitness.

Pursuing fitness brings me fulfillment, and the finishing of something, like a workout, is incredibly important. Simply put, having a workout goal and finishing it makes me feel good.

But what I've learned over the years is that physical fitness is not just about working out. Probably 75 to 80 percent is about diet and what you're putting into your body. Not everyone thinks about that, but in my experience everything that goes in my body is considered fuel. Most people look at food as pleasure, but I recircuited my thoughts years ago. As a result, I see it as fuel—and every time I put something in my mouth, I don't want it to just be regular old unleaded. I want it to be jet fuel. How will it make me better?

As you might imagine, I don't eat a lot of sugar. I don't eat bread. I have a whole regimen—not that I never deviate from it by a single bite, but I am always aware of how what I eat will affect my overall fitness. So if you see me eat a French fry and ketchup—which is really toxic, by the way—know that I've counted the cost and have a specific reason for eating that bite of junk. What I put in my body is all about how it makes me feel.

Beyond diet and your physical body, fitness is about emotional well-being. I'll speak more to that in a few pages. Suffice it to say, fitness is something our family takes very seriously. Here are a few of our guiding principles:

The Garapedian family advocates a strong, healthy diet paired with consistent exercise for everyone. (My wife is the leader there. If you come into my house looking for potato chips, you're not going to find them. We believe in whole food, not fake—processed—food.)

One of the bonds that connect our family is fitness. Life isn't always about being comfortable, especially when it comes to pushing your family athletically. Garapedians hold each other accountable for our workouts (and everyone works out).

We demonstrate leadership through fitness, whether it's racing in a triathlon or just setting an example by being the first person in a cold pool in the early morning for training. Our family puts in the work even when no one else is looking. (When I get up, get in my car, and go to the pool at 5:30 a.m., no one's watching me. I'm alone.)

Our family values mental and emotional fitness. We reflect, we meditate, and some of us participate in breath work and cold-water therapy. (My personal observation of this principle of family fitness consists of tennis, swimming, skiing, yoga, golf, mountain biking, Peloton, and circuit workouts.)

As we journey forward, the Garapedian family is dedicated to advancing our legacy of fitness as a cornerstone of our lifestyle. We will persist in leading by example, inspiring not only our own family, but also our community, to embrace fitness by fostering an environment where every challenge is an opportunity for growth. Every success is a moment for communal celebration. We aim and cultivate a future where our commitment to fitness generates in general health and happiness for the generations of the Garapedians.

HERITAGE FITNESS

Recently I had three tons of white coral sand shipped from Augusta to our house in California. I'm an avid golfer, and I have a chipping green and sand traps on our property. Part and parcel with the way I treat golf as a practice, I'm very particular about my sand and replace it every four or five years.

But I did not want the gardeners wheelbarrowing all that sand across the 30-40-yard hike from the street to the trap. I wanted to do it. In addition to saving work for my gardeners, I wanted to embrace the labor as a reminder of how hard it is to do laborious work. So, I moved that six thousand pounds of sand myself, using a wheelbarrow, over five days.

Well, not entirely by myself.

I also brought my grandkids over to help me. Why? I wanted them to put some sand in the wheelbarrow. Much like my own father bringing me into the woodshop, I wanted them to see what I was doing and embrace the work with me. They're only three and one, so really, they make more of a mess than anything. But I still wanted them there so that they could embrace the legacy of this example.

I make a practice of that—bringing my grandkids in to work (and play) beside me from time to time. The three-year-old has helped me clear leaves off the tennis court with my blower; he has helped me wash the car and dip debris out of the pool with a net. Why not sand and a wheelbarrow? Believe it or not, it was great fun.

Let me tell you—shoveling all that sand was also a great workout. But even more than that, every shovel of sand was a reminder: *It's a process. It's a process. It's a process.* It took me five days, but—as stupid as this could sound to someone else—I am so proud of that sand.

I really value my sand traps. But I value my legacy of fitness even more, and I know fitness is passed down by example.

Simply put, it's what I want for future Garapedians, and I'm doing my part to deliver it.

TWO SIDES OF THE SAME FITNESS COIN

I like to think of emotional exercise as gymnastics, or the fitness practice of making my brain sharper and stronger. That depends so much on the people I'm interacting with. If I'm around people who are stimulating and making me better, that's good for me. I don't want to be the smartest person in the room; I want to be the dumbest person in the room, because that's how I grow.

Emotional fitness is also tightly intertwined with physical fitness. Throughout my career, I pursued both in another important way: my physical fitness affected how I fit into the suits I wore to work for almost forty years, which impacted the way I saw myself—ergo, my emotional fitness.

I'll talk about my clothes in another chapter, but here I'll say that I always had a personal stylist and a personal tailor. I never purchased readymade clothes or shoes from a store. I had all my clothes, suits, and shoes made bespoke, because I really valued dressing well and feeling good. That all comes back to physical fitness in a fairly obvious way: if I'm going to purchase and enjoy putting on a nice suit, I should be able to keep my waist at the size twenty-nine or thirty it's always been.

This issue comes up often with my clients. Most men my age have significantly larger midsections, and that's their choice. It's their choice to have wine, and crackers, and all those fun indulgences that result in extra inches around your middle. I don't judge it (thanks to lots of therapy), but I do acknowledge it.

When it comes to my clients, I advocate for them. I find out what their sweet spots are, and then I prioritize acting as an advocate for their fitness because I know it's going to make them feel better. If someone asks me, "Barry, how do I look?" and wants me to be really, truly honest with them, I value that expression of trust and respect it by offering a sensitive answer.

"Bill, I could be really honest with you," I say. "I can tell you the real truth, or I can give you a fluff answer. Which would you prefer?"

Often, Hypothetical Bill will reiterate his desire for an honest answer.

"All right," I'll say. "Bill, you're a forty-inch waist and fifty pounds overweight. You can do better."

Hypothetical Bill almost always falls silent.

"I can help you," I'll continue. "First off, nothing happens until you admit that you need change. When you do, I can get you a trainer. I can get you a nutritionist. And I will tell you, you'll feel so much better. I can't do it for you—I'm your money guy. I'll help with all your finances, but you need a pro in these other areas, too. And you need to commit."

I repeat versions of this conversation over and over again, always with the person's permission to answer their question honestly. Doing that yields tremendous credibility and trust between us because I'm giving them an answer that, frankly, many people won't give. It's a heavy answer, because there are always things they don't want to hear that need to be said. But getting their permission to be totally honest helps me make them feel comfortable.

By this point, you know that's what it's all about.

In these conversations, it helps immensely to frame these heavy comments as positives. The extra fifty pounds Hypothetical Bill is carrying around can be framed as an opportunity to reduce pain in his knees and ankles.

"Bill," I'll say, "do you know what that extra weight is doing to your knees? You're talking about always having pain in your knees and ankles, and look. For every one pound you lose, you take six pounds of compression off your knees. *Six pounds.* You've been talking about having knee problems and meniscus surgery, but we can take a hundred pounds off your joints just by helping you lose that weight."

As I've said before, I'm no doctor or dietician, but I have had enough conversations with doctors and dieticians over the years to confidently tell someone that light is right. Maintaining a healthy body weight is almost necessary to maintain healthy joints and successfully engage in activities like cycling, climbing, and other sports. It's just physics.

And there's no denying that becoming physically fit will influence your emotional fitness for the better.

One last word about emotional fitness. In my experience, sometimes emotional fitness is finding a balance between your personal standards and those of the people in your life. I know my family has felt a tremendous amount of implied pressure around me because of my standards. In my career and life, I've worked very hard. So, in social settings, I'll often order the naughty desserts to help facilitate everyone feeling comfortable. I'll have a Diet Coke or a beer to blend in, and I'll even take a bite of something I would otherwise never eat, just to be a team player.

My therapist tells me I don't need to do that—I should just be myself, have my water with lemon, and let that be that. But there's nothing worse than being with a group of people who are trying to enjoy themselves around you, and you're the only one drinking water. It's not cool. So I work hard at blending in, and I'm something of a unicorn in that area.

For me, it all comes back to creating value for others. As you know, I find immense value in making the people around me feel good, comfortable, safe, and joyful. If it takes a few bites of cheesecake to accomplish that, I think it's a small price to pay for the benefit of someone else.

And there will always be future sand to shovel.

LESSON 5

FINANCIAL

In the Garapedian family, financial wisdom is not just inherited. It's cultivated through deliberate lessons and shared experiences, shaping a legacy where fiscal responsibility and generosity converge. Barry and Sharon, by example, demonstrate the importance of collaborative decision-making and the prudent management of family resources, our money. We instill in each generation the value of a dollar, the significance of hard work, and the virtues of financial claims. Our approach to finances goes beyond mere savings. It's about strategically investing in education, real estate, and personal development. Doing that, each family member has the opportunity to pursue their passions within a supportive and well-structured financial framework. This holistic perspective shapes our future generations into stewards of their own wealth.

—excerpted from the Garapedian family charter

HERE WE ARE, at the fifth F: Financial.

Given my background and career, it will come as no surprise that I think this F is huge. But perhaps what will surprise you is my approach. In my household and with my clients, I take a holistic approach to financial. Yes, we balance our checkbooks and make healthy investments. Yes, we approach discretionary spending with an eye to providing for our future.

But we think financial is so much more than money.

Consider that phrase I just used: *healthy investments*. By all means, build a diversified investment portfolio that meets your risk tolerance and builds wealth. But I encourage you to think of healthy investments the way my parents did when I was a kid, and the way I have throughout my career and as a parent by investing in personal development.

My parents invested in me by consistently providing mentors and coaches. It's incredible to me that they were able to budget so much of their paycheck to the personal development of an eight-year-old and make it possible for me to take that investment all the way into my profession.

Likewise, Garapedians invest in mentors. We are big advocates in learning technique and developing good habits early. When one of my kids wanted to play golf, they got golf lessons so that they could learn the grip and be able to play eighteen holes—just like my parents made sure I learned the proper techniques for skiing and tennis. Whatever form it takes, investing in education is huge.

Think about this: with a few exceptions for royals and aristocracy, Europeans believe in a system of merit, not entitlement. Let me repeat that. *Europeans believe in a system of merit, not entitlement.* They are not given anything except a strategy, a path, an education—the tools for *how* to earn what they want in life.

I like that. It's congruent with my beliefs about skills, advancement, and wealth. In fact, Sharon and I have worked hard to ensure our kids never developed that noxious sense of entitlement that cripples so many kids from successful families. We've been successful, and many of my clients work with me because I'm a master at knowing what's going through their entitled kid's head. I know how to decouple these kids from that entitlement and chip away the ice.

So, for the sake of this chapter, financial is all about investing in yourself and your future. It's about cultivating the habits and mindset that will empower you to live generously, peacefully, and well.

Here are a few of our family principles:

Barry and Sharon jointly make the decisions for the household. Jointly means we share and discuss major financial decisions before taking any action. (Neither of us does this individually—we intentionally do it together.)

Our family understands the value of a dollar. (Our kids worked early. We advocated. We create an atmosphere conducive to everyone finding their passion and what they excel in. Everyone has a choice to work in their chosen path, and that's very important. We didn't tell our kids what to do. "You can do anything you want to do," we said.)

Barry and Sharon are financial stewards of their wealth, passing down healthy habits to their children and grandchildren. (Healthy habits include things like moving my own sand for my sand traps.)

We make our children better versions of ourselves by educating and investing in them. (I have no problems getting kids into coaching, swim lessons, tennis lessons, or golf lessons or employing math and other subject tutors. Education, athletics, mentorship, and counseling are all worthy of investment.)

Our family has clarity and transparency in our finances. (I keep an "open book" with Sharon, and she can look at anything she wants to see. Our kids also know exactly what we have. We gauge our real measurements. If they want to look at our accounts, we simply say, "Here's what we have." We have nothing to hide.)

Save for a home. (We're big advocates for this—we organize sub accounts designated for real estate. I remember doing this for myself.

I had special savings accounts designated for property acquisition when I was younger.)

Our family does not take away from all the struggle that is necessary to be successful. (In other words, we allow healthy struggles to happen. Clearly our kids are in the "healthy struggle" phases of their lives—they're building their careers on Wall Street; they're building their businesses from the ground up. Meaning, Daddy didn't give them their book. Believe me, that's huge. They are doing it themselves and struggling in a healthy way. They're working hard, working smart, coming into the office first and leaving last.)

As we gaze into the future, the Garapedian family is committed to perpetuating our tradition of financial wisdom and stewardship, aiming to foster a legacy that thrives on prudence, merit, and collaboration. We will continue to engage in open discussions about our financial choices, and each decision is a reflection of our collective values and individual aspirations. (*Individual* is important. Everyone has their own aspirations because we empowered each family member to understand and manage finances.)

With integrity, we are setting the foundation for successful generations to inherit not only wealth, but also the skills necessary to sustain it—which is our value, our heritage. (It's not just the inheritance of this money. It's setting our grandkids up to inherit our values, our inner truths, the way we tick. I'll talk about heritage more in chapter 10, but here I'll say that my grandkids will know what's important to me because I take the time and make the effort to demonstrate all the values I hold dear. Whether it's by blowing leaves off the court, helping with the pool, washing my car, or moving sand, they'll see I value a strong, shared work ethic because I demonstrate it and make them a part of it. I did that with my own kids, and I'm already watching that heritage unfold. As I write this, I'm sixty-six, and my son is doing with his kids what I did with him.)

GETTING OUTSIDE YOUR COMFORT ZONE IN THE MOVIE OF YOUR LIFE

When we talk about mindset and the nitty-gritty of your finances, one thing always emerges: the comfort zone.

Comfort zones are…nice. They're *comfortable.* They don't challenge or push you. They don't wake you in the middle of the night with anxiety-related sweats. Which is fine, I guess, if that's your thing. But I will tell you that staying wound up in your comfort zone will never help you grow. It's too easy to get stuck there, especially if you're a person with the money and resources to make your comfort zone extra comfy.

And you may not even realize you've gotten stuck there.

The comfort zone is an easy web to get caught in. This is true for all areas of our lives, including our finances. If you're not constantly putting effort into getting outside your comfort zone—into getting *intentionally uncomfortable* so you can grow—you'll get caught.

Take your portfolio. Perhaps it's stable and earning money. It's fairly low-drama, like a rom-com—whatever tension is there will probably turn out okay. Nice, even.

But could it be better?

Now think about "portfolio" as a metaphor for life. Let's say one area of your portfolio is in stocks, and there are seven different subsets of stocks: growth, value, international, small cap, mid cap…you get the idea. If I'm your money guy, I'm going to tell you that you need at least one piece of that pie in something that's outside your comfort zone. You need to push the needle a bit farther from *rom-com* and a bit closer to *action flick.* It's just necessary. Getting into a context of different stock exposures or different investments outside of your norm could do the trick.

And to do that successfully, you need to bring in experts to help.

Case in point: I am not an expert in all investing areas. So, when I have a client who wants to invest in one of the areas in which I'm less fluent, I bring in an expert in that particular field to handle that specific investment. In the stock world, I will manage your portfolio using subsets of managers who help me make sure your investments are sound.

Again, think of a movie being made here in Hollywood. Bringing in experts sets me up as the executive producer of your money movie, so to speak. I hire the director, the lighting people, the grips, the actors, the actresses. I'm not involved in the nitty-gritty of buying and selling, or doing the research on a particular company, or what have you. I'm just in charge of the big picture.

That's what I did on Wall Street. I then found a money manager and paid him twenty-five basis points for managing a particular portfolio. That allowed me to keep seventy-five basis points to keep the entire operation running. I also had different managers running stocks, bonds...you get the idea. For each portfolio, I had ten or eleven people managing and delivering information, statistics, and recommendations to me that I could deliver to the client. I paid others to do the detailed work so I could focus on what I do best: relationships and rainmaking (finding the money and managing it). One of the sharpest tools in my kit was *knowing* what I was good at and *knowing* that other smart people should handle the parts at which I was less skilled.

You know by now that's a strategy I've deployed in multiple areas of my life. I bring the smartest people in the world around me for a particular project, goal, career move, or to develop an important skill. Because in order to really grow, you need to bring other experts in to help you. It's the who, not the how.

My advice to you is to do the same. Apply the action-flick portfolio principles to your whole life, not just your money, and get out of your comfort zone.

Be the executive producer of the movie of your life.

BE MORE COURAGEOUS AND CONFIDENT

Becoming the executive producer of your life will take courage. It'll take confidence. Many people come to me convinced that they don't have the energy to develop those qualities. But I find it takes a *lot* of energy to be scared and fearful. Why not take that same energy, reverse the current, and put it into being bold, competent, and courageous?

The beginning of courage is competence. Throughout my career in finance, I helped my clients feel more comfortable and competent in the markets with my experience and knowledge. I explained what was happening when the market was experiencing a correction; I talked them through tremendous drops in the market by educating them on market cycles. "This is absolutely natural," I would advise them. "The world's not coming apart—the market is just cyclical. Matter of fact, when it goes down a bit more, that's when we'll be buying."

Educating my clients brought them competence. It also forged a connection of trust between us. I always spoke plainly—I didn't use a fancy lexicon or jargon they didn't understand, because terms like "treasury yield" don't build confidence or help people feel good when they turn the news on and watch the market go down 20 percent. That's called a correction, and those are absolutely necessary, so I educated my clients on that aspect of being in the market. The bottom line is that I helped them understand, and more importantly, *believe*, that they were going to be okay.

My work with clients at MAG7 is very similar in that I'm often helping my clients build the kind of competence that naturally leads to confidence and courage. The principle of cycles holds true outside of the stock market. Everything is cyclical. Real estate, stocks, relationships—there are cycles to everything. And, regardless of where your challenges lie, education and strategy will always help navigate them.

Let's say you're naturally shy or reserved. How might you learn to be more courageous and confident? Call in the experts, educate yourself on the learnable skills that will help you be more outgoing, and use strategies to build your confidence in that area.

The first strategy I go to is always repetition. Simply put, there's no substitute for doing something over and over again. Repetition produces confidence. In tennis, hitting 400 forehand volleys across the court in a particular area will make you competent. When ball 401 comes at you, you can swing with confidence because you've seen this before, you've done this before, and therefore you know you can do it again. *Wham.*

In my mind, that principle applies to everything. Someone who is very uncomfortable with public speaking can become proficient if they simply script out their message, memorize it (or craft the outline of a narrative to deliver from the heart), and practice, practice, practice.

Competence is an exercise. Exercise produces confidence.

And confidence inevitably leads to courage.

HONORING YOUR CALENDAR

What does it mean to honor your calendar? At its core, it's about respecting people and respecting their time.

My time is collateral. It's currency. It's the most valuable resource I have in my day, and I use it as efficiently and effectively as possible. There are 1,440 minutes in a day. I spend 400 of them in sleep and invest 1,040 of them in my waking hours. In meetings with clients, mentors, or collaborators, I might have an hour scheduled to spend. I honor that hour because I know we're both busy. We have sixty minutes to make it work.

In other words, it's important that I structure time and energy towards that moment.

Honoring your calendar is really a strategy that works across all Seven F's. Honor your calendar to multiply your productivity at work and grow your money. Honor your calendar to multiply the time you have with your family and friends. Honor your calendar to carve out time for fun and fitness, faith and philanthropy. It works.

For anyone looking for a practical strategy for honoring their calendar, I offer mine. I usually segment my day in half-hour slots. I find that to be a good amount of time when I'm consulting because attention spans tend to wander after the thirty-minute mark (and when I'm working with kids, that period of focus is typically less than twenty minutes). Attempting to extend a call or session beyond that window is bound to bring diminishing returns—something I've been aware of for years through my work as a professional magician. *Wow your audience and quickly leave the stage* works in magic and consulting. There is a diminishing return in talking too much.

I also color code my calendar and honor the schedule I've set for myself. Over the years I've learned how to frame my calls with people so that I can have a hard stop at a certain time. I watch the clock, and when we have four minutes left, I start to wind things down. It's not robotic; I do it in a very caring, warm way. But the calendar is very important to me. If I put your name on my calendar, that's because our time is valuable. More than that, *you* are valuable. There's no way I would miss our appointment.

Ask yourself: for each of the Seven F's, what aspects are the most valuable? What will you look back and wish you'd spent more time on? Put those on your calendar.

And then honor it.

PROCESS OVER RESULTS

By now you know that I love repetition. I also love process. I like the confidence that comes from knowing there's a menu, a strategy, a collection of steps to follow that will, to a high degree of probability, yield success. That's how I taught my clients on Wall Street. "You do these things, and you'll wind up here," I'd say.

Many people fail to recognize that this is as true for investing as it is for just about anything. If you want to run a marathon, outline the process: do this, this, this, and that to prepare, and on race day, you'll be ready. If you want to bake the perfect soufflé, follow this, this, and this step with those eggs and that whisk to achieve mouth-watering results. It's the same for stocks. Purchase stock in a great company, with all its fundamentals in place, and hold it. Your stock value will grow.

The trick is to focus on process, not results. A lifetime of coaching taught me that. If I'm doing the work, I believe in my heart that I will get a good outcome. How do I know?

Because that's just the outcome of process.

BE VISIONARY

I am a huge believer in thinking big. I'm also an equally huge believer in a little-acknowledged fact: When it comes to what someone can accomplish or what their lifestyle could be like, most people *don't think big enough*. For me, it comes back to the law of attraction. Think too small, and you've diminished your outcome before you ever set out to attain it.

So, in your heart of hearts, what kind of lifestyle do you want?

Do yourself a favor and create a vision.

When it comes to my work with kids, I go back to the trusted tactic I've been using for years: creating a vision board (Tactic #8) full of images that inspire or empower them to strive. I'll talk about that in more detail below. For now, I offer a paradigm shift.

Thinking big is bigger than stuff.

Vision is bigger than money.

Dream big enough, and suddenly, you're envisioning a life of significance.

TACTICS

TACTIC #8: VISION BOARDS

I mentioned the power of imagery in the introduction, but it bears repeating here: imagery is powerful because what we see becomes what we prioritize becomes what our goals are becomes what our reality looks like. What drives us to succeed and attain is a subliminal process, itself driven by what we see.

Harness that process by creating a vision board. If you're analog and like creating something with your hands, cut aspirational pictures from magazines or print them from your phone and arrange them on a piece of posterboard, then put it somewhere you'll see it each day. If you're not into the posterboard idea, tape the pictures to your refrigerator or bathroom mirror. Pin them to a section corkboard in your office. Whatever works for you.

If you prefer a digital version, apps like Pinterest are perfect for collecting pictures in a central location. It's easy to curate your images and remove pins when they become less relevant, when your vision changes course, or when you've achieved that particular dream.

TACTIC #9: INVEST IN A WARDROBE

Not everyone has the resources to invest in a personal tailor and stylist, but I allocated funding in this area throughout my life because it created value in my career of working with affluent people. Appearance counts for a lot—if I had rolled into meetings with moneyed individuals and families looking like a bum, I would've undermined my own credibility as a financially savvy advisor.

In addition to owning nice clothes, I was fastidious about details. I dressed impeccably—my shoes were buffed, my heels weren't scuffed up, my suits were pressed…you get the idea. Perhaps you're reading this and thinking, *I don't have the money for bespoke suits from Savile Row.* That's fair. But anyone can pay attention to the details when putting together the wardrobe they do have. Anyone can go the extra mile to make sure their clothes are clean, neat, and wrinkle- and scuff-free. And you should because it demonstrates thought and respect for the people you do business with.

Let's face it—what you wear will always send a message to the people you interact with each and every day.

Make sure that message is saying the right thing.

TACTIC #10: CULTIVATE RELIABILITY HABITS

Being reliable means four practices: showing up on time, doing what you say, finishing what you start, and saying please and thank you (showing appreciation).

I learned these reliability habits from Dan Sullivan, and they clicked for me. I adopted them wholesale and have used them for twenty-five years with great results, often teaching them early in kids' lives. Show up on time. Just do it. It shows respect to the person you're there to meet by demonstrating that they are valuable and that you care for them enough to not keep them waiting. Doing what you say you will and finishing what you start build personal credibility and demonstrate you take yourself seriously enough to follow through. Taken together, saying please and thank you form the necessary cornerstone of respect.

All these combined create an energy people want to feel and be around. That's as true in business as it is in your personal life.

And you can take that to the bank.

LESSON 6

FUN

In the Garapedian family, fun is an integral and vibrant thread woven through the fabric of our daily lives, enriching every interaction and experience with a sense of joy. Whether it's embarking on an exhilarating ski trip or hosting spirited dinner parties or engaging in quiet evenings of reading and reflection, our approach to leisure is as diverse as it is meaningful. Barry's passion for mentoring and career coaching along with our collective commitment to physical well-being and personal growth reflects our belief that true enjoyment stems from activities that not only entertain, but also enhance our lives. This dynamic blend of pursuits from the athletic to the artistic, from the intellectual to the whimsical, underscores a family ethos that celebrates life in all its facets, fostering a culture where fun and fulfillment go hand in hand.

—excerpted from the Garapedian family charter

NOW FOR THE sixth F: Fun.

Fun can be anything. For me, performing magic, entertaining, and seeing faces light up is fun—as is mentoring young minds, like I do at Pepperdine University. It's just as much fun for me to help make people a better version of themselves through my work at MAG7 Consulting. It brings me energy and fills my tank.

In the Garapedian family, fun includes ski trips, Hawaiian vacations, and entertaining—we *really* love entertaining. We host dinner parties and philanthropic events at our home. Sharon cooks the best meals, and we have different themes for our home-cooked dinners several nights a week, including family dinners every Sunday. We also have a tradition of going to the movies on Friday or Saturday evenings.

Exercise brings joy to all my family members. It isn't viewed as laborious, but rather as something to look forward to. We embrace reading material that makes us better versions of ourselves. We enjoy books, handwritten notes, and awesome stationery. And with that awesome stationery, we find joy in creating and reviewing our gratitude lists.

I'll share one other principle from our family charter, one that I think sums it all up:

The Garapedian family remains dedicated to cultivating a life filled with joy, creativity, and meaningful engagement. In doing so, we aim to sustain a vibrant family culture that not only celebrates the joys of today, but also eagerly anticipates the adventures yet to come, ensuring that the Garapedian legacy of lively and enriching fun is carried forward with enthusiasm and love.

IN EVERY JOB THAT MUST BE DONE

Mary Poppins has been singing it ever since her on-screen debut in 1964, and it's as true today as it was then: find the fun in what you have to do. Create that element in every task, responsibility, and interaction, and you will change your life.

I like to gamify my day and, by extension, my career. I turn each hour into a bit of a contest—me versus the items on my calendar and the hard things I have planned. This kind of play helps me focus on "winning," making my day more enjoyable and productive.

I might create segmented contests for myself to get through my daily plan. *I need to make twenty phone calls before noon. I need to ask people for a meeting, and I need three of those today.* I create metrics for my challenges and accomplishments, and I keep track of them. At the end of the day, if I've followed my process, I've won.

And I feel good about it.

My method for gamifying my day comes from a childhood spent having fun with board games. When I was growing up, my family spent a lot of time playing them. One of my favorites was *Sorry*—I loved rolling the dice, moving the pawns, and strategizing. It naturally translated into my adult life, spilling over into my goals. Take exercise and workouts. *Today I'm going to swim 3000 yards*, I'd decide, and I would break up the distance into pieces and have fun getting a certain yardage.

I spent some time in Hawaii while writing this book and did a lot of ocean swimming while I was there. I would set my distance goals, and every time I hit 500 meters, I got a buzz from my watch. The water was so clear there that I made a game of discovering marine life below the surface. Could I find that sea turtle I'd glimpsed earlier, maybe before the next buzz? I knew he was still there, gliding around somewhere in the coral.

This kind of gamification gives the gift of presence; it keeps me very in the moment—a wonderful recipe for achievement, certainly, but also for fun.

Why? If you haven't noticed, having fun is *all about being in the moment*. It's creating a memory, a crystallized bit of time, that will last. My goal is always to create a portfolio of wildly diversified moments and memories—the treasure that comes from having fun. I don't think so much about "the week" or the mountain of tasks I must accomplish in that slice of time. I do have a weekly plan, of course, but I'm far more focused on breaking my day down into sections and hours and strategizing how to have fun with each of them.

Now I'm going to let you in on a little secret: *Having fun is an outright decision.* I decided the day I wrote that last sentence that I was going to have a lot of fun. If you talked with me today, I would have already made the same decision. I'm going to maximize my day, strategize my day, and make it as perfect and great as I can.

Great, you may be thinking, *I want in. But how?* I leverage my calendar to create fun. I make sure I have enough time scheduled for breaks, so I'm not going eight straight hours on the phone or talking to people over Zoom. I'll schedule an hour of tennis with a friend here, an hour of swimming there, or slot in some lifting and ab work (which I also make fun by listening to audiobooks while working out).

Having fun is so important because it makes us happy and positive. And since people like to be around others who are having fun, it helps people want to be around us.

How can that not benefit your career? Your family? Your overall life?

ENERGY MANAGEMENT

Energy management is about my energy specific to my time. Time management is an important skill, and a lot of people home in on it. But you're simply not going to get as far if time is your only focus.

Enter *energy management*: my means for controlling my time (and my very structured calendar).

Think of it this way. If I don't have the energy to sustain me through my day, what does it matter that I have my time perfectly parceled out? I can plan a great road trip full of hotels, sightseeing, restaurants, and activities, but if I don't have enough gas in the car to get all the way down the road, that plan is worthless.

Energy management reverts to diet, water intake, and the people in my life. I keep very few individuals around me who are toxic or negative (those people I think of as "angry elves"). Why? Aside from all the obvious benefits of surrounding myself with positivity, I want to be around people I can empower—people who fill my tank instead of carving a little hole at the bottom to drain it.

Often, the people who fill my tank are people I can have fun with. In fact, it's safe to say it always goes back to having fun for me. Very few people I know prioritize fun this way, but I think we could all be more successful if we did.

FUN AND VALUE CREATION

How does fun create value? Simple: it's contagious.

Case in point. If I'm at a function or dinner and find myself sitting at a round table with ten other people in a ballroom of 200, I elect myself the leader of the table. "Okay, guys," I'll say, often interrupting the chitchat, "hold that thought and give me a minute. On the count of three, we're going to do a loud *yahoo* so that everyone else in the room can hear us." Before long, we're screaming, "Yahoo!" and everyone else in the room is looking at us and saying, "My god, those guys are having fun." It usually isn't long before an answering *yahoo* rings out across the ballroom.

People like to have fun, especially at events where they have to get dressed up. Very few are there to talk about business, so let's *have fun*. Kick it off with my Tactic #13: Going First and start asking people around you to tell you about their families. "Where do you like to vacation?" you could ask. "What do you like to do when you're not being so successful?"

Maybe you're not at an event. Maybe you're at a restaurant, grabbing lunch. Get to know your server's name and get to know *them*—in a casual, natural way, of course (I'm not recommending the Spanish Inquisition here).

The point is, make it fun for yourself by making it fun for others.

TACTICS

TACTIC #11: DOPAMINE + SOMETHING HARD = FUN

Throughout my career, I have always differentiated myself by pairing hard things with a dopamine action to create fun. Take my earlier example of having to make twenty phone calls in a day. I would pair that hard thing (making twenty calls) with a contest (a dopamine action) so that when I finished, I felt good. Essentially, "winning" the "contest" injected fun into the entire process.

The pairing is where the magic lies.

Pairing hard things with dopamine actions is a strategy for creating fun. I recommend setting a specific metric you need to hit, a goal that you find fun to reach for. It can be as simple as *Oh, I need to be at ten calls by 9:00 a.m.? Let's do this. Fifteen calls by 11:00 a.m.? Watch me get there by 10:30.*

And, like all the strategies and tactics in this book, this one applies to everything. When I'm at the gym I turn elements of my workouts into a race against the clock, using what I call minute-on-minute workouts. I challenge myself to complete seven specific exercises within two minutes (the hard thing). I play music the whole time (the dopamine act). Put those two things together, and suddenly, burpees and lunges are fun.

Another example of pairing dopamine with a hard thing is making hard things a reward. I might position myself for that if I'm doing something challenging—say, swim 18,000 yards in a week. I'll pair a dopamine act with that challenge and give myself some kind of *attaboy* when I'm done.

TACTIC # 12: CREATING LIGHTNING STRIKES

The definition of a lightning strike is *exceeding someone's expectations on purpose.* Essentially, you're creating a "wow" moment—one that brings joy and happiness.

And I say *make it fun.*

Creating a special moment that makes someone happy will inevitably bring you positive feelings and make you happy, too. I know from experience. Secretly washing someone's car when they're not looking, or choosing a random stranger at a restaurant and paying their bill, or surreptitiously buying coffee for the third person in line behind you at Starbucks and then lingering in the area to watch their reaction. Spoiler alert: it'll be wonderful.

Creating a lightning strike doesn't require spending a lot of money. The point is to create emotional and spiritual value for someone else by unexpectedly exceeding their expectations.

The simple truth is that good things happen when you do things for other people. It's counterintuitive for most—people tend to be wired to do things for themselves first. That's fine, but you'll get more bang for your buck when you put others' needs and wants before your own. That's not to say you should do it to get something in return. Emphatically, do *not* do it to get something in return. Yes, performing an act of kindness for someone else can be very strategic, but creating a lightning strike isn't about reciprocity.

And it's simply *better* to do it for fun.

LESSON 7

FILANTHROPY

In the Garapedian family, philanthropy is a vibrant expression of our collective sphere and commitment to service that is deeply ingrained in every aspect of our lives. Each family member is encouraged to engage in philanthropic activities that resonate with their passions. Whether it involves mentoring young minds or enhancing our Pepperdine community through various initiatives, our home often becomes a hub for gatherings that champion these causes. Reflecting our leadership role in fostering community spirit and cooperation, everyone in the family should be involved in some philanthropic organizations they are passionate about, whether that is serving on a board or simply donating money or time. We invest in our Pepperdine community. We celebrate their athletic programs, social speaking engagements, fraternities, business fraternities, send-off parties, and career coaching programs.

—excerpted from the Garapedian family charter

THE SEVENTH AND final F is philanthropy–or, as we like to say it, *Filanthropy*.

In business, philanthropy often translates into a sort of well-intentioned quid pro quo—a means to a specific end, like a tax write-off, that benefits the giver while also helping to alleviate suffering in some area. If that sounds negative or cynical, it isn't meant to be. At the end of the day, that system of quid pro quo ensures people and corporations who can give the most continue to do so and that people who are suffering continue to receive aid. Win-win.

I can think of situations where philanthropy opened up many doors. It has put me in conversations with others that helped me further my career, either by providing opportunities to take a look at someone's portfolio or recommending they speak with another expert. Perhaps most of all, philanthropy has often put me in a position to ask questions and be curious, which in turn helped me create value for someone and change their life.

All of that is good. Great, even.

But those are the results of philanthropy, not philanthropy itself.

It probably won't surprise you at this point to know that my definition for philanthropy is less about dollars and cents and more about an attitude, mindset, and lifestyle centered around generosity. Giving doesn't mean I have to write a check all the time. That's usually the first thing that comes to mind when we think of philanthropy, right? There's nothing wrong with writing a check. I've done it before; maybe you have, too. But I don't find it nearly as gratifying as giving human collateral to help someone.

What I mean is that I would rather spend twenty minutes on the phone, talking someone through a solution to their pain point or connecting them with someone who can help better than I can, than to write a thousand-dollar check. Checks can help, but don't they just…feel a little cold? Trust me when I say I give (and get) a lot more value when I share the warmth of human collateral by digging into where someone is hurting, sharing any wisdom I can, and helping them toward a solution.

In other words, my version of philanthropy is a mindset shift. Giving *can* refer to providing materially for someone, but materiality isn't the whole picture. To me, giving means creating the three different types of value I've been talking about all along: material, emotional, and spiritual. It means showing up to every conversation, interaction, and opportunity with a heart wholly committed to generosity.

Often philanthropy is just the little things, like never getting in the buffet line first or making sure the people who will be cleaning the dishes after the meal get to fill their plates ahead of you. Micro actions like that can make such a difference for someone (not to mention, they also demonstrate philanthropic leadership to others). They might not seem like much in the grand scheme of things, but they add up.

And when they're an outpouring of an authentically generous spirit, they're transformative.

That's what philanthropy means for me: transforming lives by choosing, each and every day, to be a giver instead of a taker. And look—we each decide early on (consciously or unconsciously) that we're either one or the other. Takers are obvious—you know who these people are. They're always wanting more of this, more of that, always receiving value but never bringing it. They never do anything to help you. On the other hand, being a giver simply means generosity—giving all of your heart to someone, all of yourself to someone, as freely and as often as you can.

Designate yourself as a giver through your words and actions, and you'll see a shift. Everyone in your life, including you, will be better for it. You'll help other people and assist them along their journey to becoming who they want to be. And in the end, helping others will help you. It might sound counterintuitive, but that's the law of the universe. That's just the way it works.

Being a giver, helping other people, and creating value is absolutely the narrative of my life. I know that means sometimes people will take advantage of me. I expect that and I accept it. If you find that statement challenging, that's because it is. In today's world, we're wired to be vigilant self-protectors. We pull ourselves up by our bootstraps and defend what's ours, right? Maybe. But I'm telling you that true generosity can make exceptions for all sorts of challenges and provide many forms of help, even ones that might not make sense on the surface.

Here are a few more of my family's philanthropic principles:

I personally mentor and share my experience with anyone who is willing to learn, helping them to blossom and grow. We teach our children the idea of paying it forward, showing them how to give to others.

We are leaders in our community. We host events at our home for organizations that we support.

Always thank a veteran, a police officer, a fireman for their service. We show gratitude to public service, whether it's police, firefighters, or teachers. (That is a regular practice in the Garapedian family. Our kids were taught early on to walk up to a police officer, fireman, or someone who is clearly a veteran and thank them for their service.)

We also move forward. As we move forward, the Garapedian family is fully committed to expanding our philanthropic endeavors, continuously seeking new ways to make meaningful difference in the community and beyond. By nurturing a deep-rooted culture of generosity and active involvement, we aim to foster lasting impact that transcends our own family. We want our immediate actions to cultivate a broader network of compassion and support. In this future, the Garapedian family's dedication to philanthropy will not only shape our own legacy but also kindle a beacon of hope, demonstrating the transformative power of generosity across generations and communities.

When you really think about it, every part of philanthropy discussed in our family charter centers around helping people. For Garapedians, it's a habit—just something we do because it's part of our DNA.

And it has worked for us. Sharon and I hear stories about our kids' philanthropic activity all the time. I heard from someone the other day that my son attended a party, but instead of merely enjoying the festivities, he jumped in and took charge when he saw a need. He designated himself as the go-to, helpful person that anyone could come to for anything that day.

In other words, he was a giver.

We often hear, "Make a difference in people's lives." I truly believe a lot of us want to take up that mantra and follow it, but we often don't know how. I'm here to tell you the first step is always getting to know the person you want to help. Find out who they are, where they are, what's going on in their life. Be curious. Then think about how you can be a giver and create value that is specific to the person.

To my mind that's a very outside-of-the box way of helping, but I have always liked to disrupt in a positive way. I'm structured, I have processes, and I'm very aware of the parameters of the box—and I'm intentional about reaching outside it to create value for others.

Make it your goal to do the same. Practice philanthropy every day.

TACTICS

TACTIC #13: PRACTICE GOING FIRST

This is an exercise I often give to the young people I work with who are (roughly) between the ages of fourteen and thirty. Going First is exactly what it sounds like: a strategy for being the first to initiate a conversation with someone, introduce yourself, say good morning, smile at someone, run over to pick up the first piece of trash…you get the idea. It's one exercise that's very easy to do and that builds a lot of confidence. It also demonstrates leadership by example.

I'll never forget a day in 2018, when I was sitting in the Burbank airport with Sharon. I had a salad balanced in my lap as I watched other travelers pass us by. The passenger terminal in the Bob Hope Airport in Burbank is relatively small—essentially one long hallway flanked by a string of gates on one side and a few shops and restrooms on the other. Anyone departing or arriving from a gate at the end of the terminal has to walk right past everyone else waiting for their flights.

So there I was, eating my salad and enjoying Sharon's company, when suddenly, from the crush of passers-by, a scream rang out. An elderly lady had fallen down in the middle of the thoroughfare. Her papers scattered all over the place.

Then something amazing happened.

Before I'd fully realized what was happening, Sharon had jumped out of her seat beside me, rushed to where the woman had fallen, and was cradling her head in her lap and giving her water. The woman was injured, and Sharon was the first person to help.

Eventually, others came to help, and Sharon returned to her seat. I was ashamed I hadn't been the first to jump up; I usually am, but my wife beat me that time. I was also bursting with pride for her.

"Honey," I said, "what makes you do that?"

"It's the way I'm wired," she answered.

I've learned so much from her about being first to help.

Remember, the point of a relationship is to relate. We do that in part by making each other better, but someone always has to take the first step.

If you let it, Going First can grow into something like a philosophy for good living. What if you use it to consistently be the first person to help someone who needs it? How might that transform your life and the lives of people around you?

TACTIC #14: PROFILES OF SUCCESS

This particular tactic involves a few steps. It works with young minds and adults alike.

To begin, I instruct my client to make a list of the twenty-five most successful people in their community or area of work. Let's say I'm coaching someone who is interested in supply chain logistics. I would have them make a list of twenty to twenty-five amazing businesses in that area that are run by only one person. I would then have my client call each of those twenty-five people for an interview, so they can learn how they reached that pinnacle of success. "Learn their story," I say. "Find out where they came from and how they got where they are."

After each interview, I tell my client to take what they learned and write a 1200–1500-word profile of that person. Yes, they write twenty-five descriptions for twenty-five different people. I collect their profiles, put them all together in one volume, and suddenly my client is the author of a book called *Profiles of Success*.

I've also used this tactic with adults in a particular industry to help them meet really successful salespeople, marketing people, business-people, students, you name it—and it works. It's also a value-creating strategy, resulting in two or three or four wonderful networking contacts for the writer. It helps them meet people they normally would not.

This tactic accomplishes a few things. First, it gets my client (the writer) out meeting those successful people. Second, the book will be used as a tool to help others when I instruct the writer to pass it on to someone they know who wants to grow in their lives. That also makes it a philanthropic tactic—one that will provide the writer with a strategy to become a better version of themselves. He or she can do the work knowing they're doing something for the greater good.

PART 3

WHAT IT'S ALL ABOUT

DELIVERING TRUE
LEGACY TO YOUR FAMILY

THE CULMINATION OF the Seven F's is the ultimate success: delivering true legacy to your family. What will that look like for you? Have you thought it through? Perhaps you know precisely. Perhaps you don't, and that's why you picked up this book. Either way, I encourage you to begin envisioning your future legacy. And don't forget to dream big.

First, take a moment and think back on your life. What legacies did you inherit? How did those legacies come to you? What legacies do you hope to leave behind? What are you doing to make sure they last?

Legacy is what Mom and Dad taught my sister and I about how to live our own lives and how to treat other people. They invested not only in lessons and mentorship for us but also in "time in the saddle," or quality time. In fact, Mom didn't start her teaching career until my sister and I were in our early teens because she felt it was important to stay home and raise us. (She then went out, got her teaching degree, and taught elementary school.)

Mom and Dad were tuned into kids. More specifically, they were tuned into giving my sister and me the best childhood imaginable. We were sheltered from negativity and toxicity—protected by the very strong metaphorical walls Mom and Dad put up around us—but also encouraged to get to know the world and experience its wonders.

In my house, leadership by example ruled the day. Mom and Dad didn't just teach us with words; they taught us by experience. The year I was in fifth grade they took us traveling around the continental United States in a camper. We hiked Yosemite and Yellowstone, learning the practical skills that come with camping such as how to build a fire and cut kindling. We also visited as many states as we could in the most American way possible—by driving. From Oklahoma to Texas to Ohio, had experiences both novel and wondrous: the sound of locusts in Texas, the sight of fireflies hovering over summer grass in Missouri, the weight of humidity hanging over a lake in Ohio.

That last one was especially memorable. There we were, in the midst of seeming paradise. But it was deserted. "How come no one's out on the lake?" I asked.

We soon found out. The minute we set foot outside, we were swarmed by hungry mosquitos.

Certainly, Mom and Dad left us with a rich legacy of happy memories and a taste for adventure and exploration. But as I've said, we also had gigs, such as learning to play an instrument early in childhood, which taught us the discipline and structure of practicing.

In other words, my parents did everything in their power to equip us for success, and it worked. My sister achieved a 4.0 GPA and was her high school valedictorian; she went on to earn her doctoral degree from the London School of Economics. And me, well, you know all about me. My skill set is different from hers, but I earned my success all the same.

What our parents invested in us was so much more than fireflies and campfires and a healthy respect for practice and structure. They instilled in us something irreplaceable: *confidence*. And I don't mean a shallow "you can be whatever you want to be" kind of confidence that fractures once you hit the real world. I'm talking about the iron-clad kind—the kind that can only come from knowing the skills and practices you need to succeed are *already built into the stuff of who you are.*

Every time Mom and Dad encouraged me with a "We believe in you," or a "We know you can do it," I believed them. When they said, "You're better than this—you can do it," I knew it was true. When you hear that from your parents over and over and over again, even before your skill set and structure and affinity for practice has taken root, you actually start to believe it.

Mom and Dad's words and actions gave me tremendous confidence early in my life. I was five, six, seven years old and doing magic shows onstage in front of my family or playing the piano at recitals in front of hundreds of people. When I think about that, it's kind of incredible. And that same confidence continues to serve me well, not only in my career, but in important moments like my daughter's recent wedding when I was able to get onstage and speak for four or five minutes, sharing stories and memories that came straight from the heart.

That's their true legacy—a heritage that's so much more than inheritance.

HERITAGE OVER INHERITANCE

Many of my clients are predominantly focused on passing down financial wealth and assets. Maybe that describes you too. Here's the thing, though: you could leave millions of dollars for your kids, and if they haven't cultivated the right values, all that wealth could disappear in the blink of an eye. Worse, it could disappear because it's being used to fuel substance abuse or another debilitating habit. It pains me to admit that narrative is an unfortunately common one in affluent families.

It's also one of the many reasons I encourage you to focus on *heritage* over *inheritance.*

Heritage over inheritance means leaving your children and grand-children with more than just money and cold assets. It means leaving them with a wealth of values that they can pay forward to future generations—the qualities that will empower their future success.

Great, you may be thinking. *How do I do that?*

I'm glad you asked. The first thing you absolutely *must* do is spend quality time with your family. My parents drove me across the US. I bring my grandkids to help me shovel sand for my bunkers and spend hours playing in the pool or building sandcastles with them when we're in Hawaii. The activity itself doesn't matter as much; the point is just *being with them*. Effectively passing down your values, principles, inner truths is a feat that requires leadership by example, which you can only do if you're *there*. That's just how heritage over inheritance happens.

The second thing you must do is answer an important question: do you *articulate* the values and inner truths that you want to pass down? A lot of my clients answer that question with, "No, but I have them in my head." That's a good starting place, but I'm here to tell you it's not enough. If your values are in your head, how do you pass them down?

That brings me to the third thing you need to do: put your values *on paper*. That's where having your own family charter comes in (and where my services at MAG7 can help).

When someone comes to our house and knocks on the door, my son or daughter will answer and introduce themselves. They'll shake hands with the person and invite them to please come in and sit down. They'll offer something to drink. Those are manners, yes, but they're also the values that Sharon and I taught our family. Everyone knows manners exist, but the trick is getting your children to *value* them.

Otherwise, they'll be lost in a single generation.

KEEPING HERITAGE THROUGH THE THIRD GENERATION

Making sure your values aren't lost by the third generation is largely up to you. To put it bluntly, you have to make the choice to pass down your values and follow up with a written family charter and a plan for executing it. Then follow your plan.

You could wing it, but that's not going to be as good or effective. You absolutely need the structure of a written charter or constitution. That's not to say you're establishing a set of laws, and you have to start running around like a policeman enforcing them. Just know what you want, write it down, and have a structure for gifting those good values to your kids.

There should be a bit of strategy in how you pass them down. More than anything, it's about having the *intent* (one that goes beyond just showing up) to craft a lasting legacy and heritage.

Notice I just used the word *craft*. A lasting heritage isn't instantaneous. It takes a lifetime of dedication and practice. So, in those years of practicing your values, demonstrate them for your kids like my parents did for me. Reflect them in your actions. Use Tactic #5 and tell good stories that double down on your point.

In fact, I can't stress enough that good storytelling is crucial to lasting heritage. I can tell my grandkids how they should respond to all sorts of situations that happen in the real world. But it'll be far more effective—not to mention enjoyable for everyone involved—to teach them how the world works by inventing stories about that sea turtle I saw while ocean swimming in Hawaii. "There are whole worlds down there in the water," I might say, "full of enemies and ecosystems and a million billion wonderful things."

I know that technique works because I remember going to the beach year after year and building incredible sandcastles with my mom. And do you know what happened? Each time we went back, she reinforced and built on our family history, heritage, and values with a simple, "Do you remember when…?"

Practically speaking, that simple question is just one of many entry points into a story—one she used to make sure I would remember. Like I said at the beginning of this book, values and principles on a wall oftentimes aren't remembered, but a story is. Why? Because stories connect. They get their hooks in us, in the best possible way, and don't let go.

Lace your stories with your legacy, and your kids and grandkids will remember.

And they will keep your heritage *alive*.

TACTICS

TACTIC #15: THE BOOKS WE READ, THE PEOPLE WE MEET

The books you read, the people you meet is my mantra. I have a goal every month to read two different books, for a total of twenty-four books in a year.

I've learned so much from books. They make me a better person, increase my lexicon, my vocabulary, my perspectives. Want to be a better storyteller? Read more books. Looking at different words in a book will sharpen your skills. The way something is described could even set your imagination spinning, helping you see something or learn about it in a new way. The ability to read books is absolutely a treasure. And if you're not a natural reader, use Audible, or some other form of audiobooks, and *read with your ears*.

Much of the same can be said about the people you meet. They oftentimes make me a better Barry. I always approach interactions with someone new from a place of curiosity. How did they become so successful? What do they do for fun? Where do they like to travel? What sports or activities are they involved in? Where did they go to college? And on and on. My goal is always to get them to talk about themselves because maybe I can learn something from them. Maybe something they're doing could help me be a better version of myself.

TACTIC #16: CREATING A PERSONAL ADVISORY BOARD

For many years, I was a member of many boards. Somewhere along the line, I thought it could be great if I created a board for myself—an advisory committee that would help keep me on track in my goal of becoming a better Barry.

Just like that, the personal advisory board was born.

I recommend this tactic to my clients, both adults and kids. When I pitch this idea to kids, I frame it in terms of superpowers. "Think about the superpower you have," I might say, "and now think about the superpowers you don't have but wish you did. Which of your friends or other people in your life have them?"

Maybe the kid has a real gift in the faith department but lacks the commitment or drive for fitness. Luckily for him, his best friend is an athlete—fitness is his superpower and therefore would be a great addition to my client's personal advisory board.

I recommend meeting for thirty minutes, either in person or over video chat so that the board can check in with my client as he strives to cultivate their superpowers. Like any organizational or corporate board, they're there to provide accountability as the client tries to achieve certain goals.

Let's say a kid wants to develop a high-performance habit that needs to be done every single day. Their board is there to make sure that's happening and offer encouragement or find a better approach when it isn't. But perhaps the biggest benefit for that kid is knowing they're not alone in their pursuit. There are people who really care about them and love them enough to help them become a better person.

We break these meetings up into ninety-day sessions that focus on a single aspect of improvement. I emphasize calls to action paired with real activities that they actually do. And I can tell you from experience that it's amazing to watch their progress. It's incredible to see what these kids gain.

TACTIC #17: THINKING BIG

I refer to thinking big as a kind of philosophy for life throughout this book, but it's a strategy just as much as it's a philosophy. Intentionally use Thinking Big to grow your dreams and free yourself to do more.

Many times through the years, I've seen people thinking too small, and do you know what happens? They minimize what they can do. That's right. I've seen this in financial advisors, entrepreneurs, and friends. The first way to put limits on your abilities and successes is to have small dreams, small goals, and small beliefs in what you can accomplish.

In my experience, that all starts when we're young.

Sadly, so many small dreamers came to their limiting beliefs when they were kids. Think about the ones you've met, and you'll know exactly what I'm talking about. Those kids who lack confidence—even to the point of often feeling fearful—will continue to experience small thinking and limitations.

That's not to say confidence and courage can't be learned later in life, but it will be a whole lot harder. Look at it this way: mastering martial arts when you're a kid is much easier than it is when you're fifty or sixty years old. So the trick is to master that positive mindset as early as possible.

If this is news to you, start now.

Right this minute.

And, if you're a parent or a mentor figure for young minds, start those kids out on a solid foundation of thinking big. Trust me when I say you'll put them light-years ahead by doing so.

Training those young minds starts with leadership—yours, a teacher's, a coach's, all of the above. Everyone's in a different place. I know because that's what my mom and dad did for me. We came from a middle-class family, and when my parents shared a bigger vision for my life with me, those big dreams took root.

I dreamed of becoming a businessman, and by junior high, I was carrying a black attaché case instead of a backpack, all my pens and calculators and folders neatly aligned inside. By high school, I was dressing for success too—and you better believe I got "Best Dressed" my senior year.

In other words, my big dreams gave me the confidence to emulate the life I wanted. Collectively, they were the cornerstone of all the practices, protocols, and road maps I developed to reach my vision of success.

And it all worked.

I have a button I've had for many years that says, "I believe." The idea is, you simply push it when you need to believe in yourself. It's a straightforward little gimmick, but it does something incredible. Every time I push that button, I'm making a declaration: I believe. And every time I say it, real belief follows.

My challenge to you is this: think bigger than you ever have before, and then hit that metaphorical button and declare your belief. Teach your kids to dream big and believe in themselves early on too. Use it for everything—from dreams for a beautiful home or lifestyle to building foundations and helping the underserved. Remember, what you can do for someone else depends on how much you believe in you.

If you need help getting started, pair this tactic with Tactic #8: Vision Boards, and see where your dreams can take you.

TACTIC #18: WIN THE MORNING

I use this tactic all the time—literally every day. It's applicable for just about everyone.

The narrative here is that if I win the morning, I'll win the day. Here's another way to phrase that: What specifically am I doing in the morning to win my day?

For starters, I honor my alarm clock. That means I don't hit the snooze button. I take a cold shower and have all my toiletries already laid out in the bathroom. I follow a personal morning protocol that includes sit-ups, push-ups, and planking for ninety seconds. All in all, my exercise and getting ready combined take a reliable forty-five minutes, and then I'm off to the races.

But winning the morning doesn't stop when I'm dressed and out the door. There are specific practices I continue to do throughout the day. I never listen to sports in the morning or do anything socially; everything is task-oriented and business-centric. And I already have my plan for the day written down—who I'm calling, what time, and for how long. All my structures are in place so I can simply enter the process and build momentum as the day rolls on, which really puts me in the right place mentally *and* physically.

Perhaps you noticed that I said my toiletries were *already* laid out and my plan for the day was *already* in place. That's the secret to winning the morning.

It starts the evening before.

Evening prep begins with organizing everything I'll need for the next day so I can get excited about how it will unfold. Toiletries, schedules, eating right (if I'm not eating the right foods, it's not good). All of it gets taken care of before I go to bed.

Then I *go to bed.* At a decent, even early, hour.

I do all of that to make sure that when my alarm goes off at 4:00 a.m., I will be ready to roll with a good, positive mindset and genuine excitement for the day.

CONCLUSION

CONNECTING

MY SISTER, CARLA, read an early draft of this book. Afterward, she called me. "Barry, this entire book can be boiled down to one thing," she said. "It's all about connecting." I told you she's brilliant.

People ask me all the time, "Barry, what is winning? Really?" The answer I always give is this: winning—true winning—is learning these seven lessons they never taught you in school, and then using my 18 Tactics to implement those lessons into your life and connect with others. Do this, and I promise you'll gain clarity and become a better version of yourself.

But remember, you become that 2.0 version of yourself *by helping other people get where they want to be.*

That is truly what's important. Help others get where they want to be, and do it through the art of *connecting*. Notice I didn't say, "Help people get where they want to be through communicating." No. Communication can be lots of things, including clear and easy, without inspiring true connection. And that's what we're after, folks. Like Carla said, *connecting* is what it's all about.

Remember, too, that connecting doesn't require spending a lot of money. It doesn't require an elaborate setup. While I was writing this chapter, one of my clients' mothers had a birthday. Her name is Kelly, and she's an avid tennis player like me. I knew her birthday was coming up, so I decided to have a little fun.

I went outside to my home tennis court and used my iPhone to film a leaf floating down from the sky and getting caught in the net. Then I walked closer and closer to the leaf, zooming in...and in... and in a little more, until the leaf's detail was crystal clear onscreen. Earlier, I'd written the words, "Happy birthday, Kelly!" on that leaf, and I focused in on the message for a few moments before ending the video and texting it to her early on the morning of her birthday.

All that gesture really took was some foresight and a small bit of planning on my part. It was simple. I needed a pen, a leaf, and my smartphone. From start to finish, it took fifteen minutes of my day, and I had fun doing it. And do you know what happened?

Kelly texted me.

"Barry," she said, "I have never seen anything like this. It's so memorable and so thoughtful. I will never forget it."

Creating that kind of lightning strike for someone is what my method can help you do.

I challenge you to take this book for what it is: an invitation to dream up the life you've always wanted, paired with a collection of proven templates and strategies to implement in your day-to-day as you make that dream your reality. Use this tool to create a plan for building the routine, the relationships, and the healthier, stronger version of yourself that will enrich you personally and improve the lives of those around you.

As you do that, I also challenge you to deploy my 18 Tactics to genuinely and authentically *connect* with others. You'll help them feel good, and you'll feel good in the process. And with each small step in that direction, you'll get closer and closer to that better version of yourself. Whether you get there by being a better storyteller, winning the morning, creating a vision board, or all of the above, you can have that life you've dreamed up.

Use this book, and you *can* win the game of life.

BONUS TACTIC #19: CONTACT BARRY

Creating a family charter is a significant step toward intentionally building that better life and creating heritage for your loved ones. Your family already has inner truths; why not write them down? Why not pursue them intentionally? Why not go after that life you want *right now*?

So I leave you with one final, bonus tactic: if you're curious about how I can help through coaching, consulting, or creating a custom charter and coat of arms for your family, reach out to me at Barry@ mag7consultants.com or by scanning the QR code on this page.

Because I would love to help *you*.

ACKNOWLEDGMENTS

ANY SUCCESSFUL ENTREPRENEUR knows that there are more people than you can count who have contributed to and inspired any sort of lasting success.

Here is my list:

My wife Shay-Shay, my daughter Missy Lou, my son Scotty, my mom Virginia, my dad Leo, my sister Carla, my son-in-law Jordan, my sister-in-law Ruby, Al Lavery, Richard Day, Dan Sullivan, Jon Powell, John Bowen, Rocky Lang, Bill Bachrach, Joe Polish, Bob Castellini, John Drabeck, Ken Larson, and Edith and Juan Perlo.

ABOUT THE AUTHOR

BARRY GARAPEDIAN, A visionary in finance and family legacy planning, brings nearly four decades of expertise to his role as founder of MAG7 Consulting. His distinguished career as a managing director at a major wire house earned him national recognition from the *Financial Times* and *Barron's*.

A USC graduate with a BA in public policy, Barry's diverse background includes performing magic at the iconic Magic Castle, teaching tennis, and participating in Ironman triathlons. His guiding philosophy that life is about the books you read and the people you meet underscores his dedication to lifelong learning and creating meaningful connections.